RENAL DIET COOKBOOK

3000+ Days of Low Potassium, Sodium and Phosphorus No Fuss, Delicious Recipes; Learn how to Master your Chronic Kidney Disease with 60 Days Flexible Meal Plan

RACHEL J. DAVIDSON

Table of Content

INTRODUCTION

Welcome to your guide to cooking great meals for a renal diet! Renal diets are designed to help people with kidney disease manage their condition and keep their kidneys functioning properly. Through this cookbook, you'll learn how to make delicious meals that are both healthy and tailored to the needs of a renal diet. With easy to follow recipes, helpful nutrition tips, and nutritional breakdowns for each dish, you'll be able to make mouth watering meals that will benefit your health and well being. So get your apron on, and let's get cooking!

CHAPTER 1:
DEVELOPING A RENAL DIET PLAN

In this chapter, we will discuss how to develop a renal diet plan to help manage kidney disease. We will look at the types of foods to include and avoid, as well as meal planning tips.

Eating a healthy diet is one of the most important steps to managing kidney disease. A renal diet is specifically designed to limit certain foods and beverages to help reduce the number of waste products that accumulate in the blood. This type of diet is generally low in sodium, phosphorus, and potassium, and is often high in protein.

When developing a renal diet plan, it is important to talk to your doctor or a registered dietitian. They can provide you with personalized advice and help you create a plan that meets your needs.

Types of Foods to Include

When creating a renal diet plan, it is important to include a variety of healthy foods. Some foods to consider include

Fruits and vegetables: Aim to include a variety of fruits and vegetables into your diet. Some examples include apples, oranges, bananas, broccoli, spinach, and carrots.

Protein: Protein is important for maintaining muscle mass and strength, and can be found in a variety of foods. Choose lean sources of protein such as eggs, fish, and legumes.

Low sodium dairy products: Dairy products can be high in phosphorus and sodium, so be sure to choose low sodium varieties. Examples include low sodium cottage cheese and yogurt.

Whole grains: Whole grains contain fiber and other nutrients that are important for maintaining a healthy diet. Examples include quinoa, brown rice, and oats.

Low sodium condiments and spices: Condiments and spices can add flavor to your meals without adding too much sodium. Choose low sodium varieties of condiments such as mustard, ketchup, and hot sauce.

Types of Foods to Avoid

When following a renal diet plan, there are certain foods that should be avoided. These include:

High sodium processed foods: Processed foods such as canned soups, frozen dinners, and deli meats are often high in sodium, phosphorus, and potassium.

High potassium fruits and vegetables: Foods such as potatoes, bananas, and oranges are high in potassium and should be avoided.

High sodium condiments: Condiments such as soy sauce, steak sauce, and salad dressings are often high in sodium.

Alcohol: Alcohol can be damaging to the kidneys and should be avoided.

Tips for Meal Planning

When creating a renal diet plan, it is important to plan out your meals for the week. This will help ensure that you are eating a balanced diet and avoiding foods that should be restricted. Here are some tips for meal planning:

Make a list: Start by making a list of the foods you will be eating throughout the week.

Plan meals in advance: Plan out meals for breakfast, lunch, and dinner for the entire week. This will help you make sure that you are eating a balanced diet.

Cook in bulk: Cook large batches of food and store them in the fridge or freezer for easy reheating throughout the week.

Be creative: Get creative with your meals and find new recipes to try.

By following these tips and including the right types of foods in your diet, you can create a renal diet plan that will help you manage your kidney disease.

CHAPTER 2:
THE BENEFITS OF RENAL DIET

The renal diet is an incredibly important part of managing kidney disease and can have a direct impact on your health and quality of life. A renal diet is specifically designed to help manage kidney disease, as it restricts certain foods which can worsen kidney function. The diet also helps to control your blood pressure, cholesterol levels, and other important factors which can be impacted by kidney disease.

The renal diet can be incredibly beneficial for those suffering from kidney disease. Here are some of the key benefits of following a renal diet:

1. Maintaining Healthy Blood Pressure: High blood pressure can be very dangerous and can further damage your kidneys. A renal diet helps to keep your blood pressure at a healthy level by avoiding foods which can cause it to spike.

2. Aiding in Weight Loss: A renal diet can be a great help in losing weight. Many of the foods which are restricted on the diet are high in calories and unhealthy fats, so eliminating them can help you to reach your weight loss goals.

3. Managing Cholesterol Levels: Cholesterol is another factor which can be impacted by kidney disease. A renal diet helps to keep your cholesterol levels in check by focusing on foods which are low in saturated fat and cholesterol.

4. Reducing Symptoms of Kidney Disease: A renal diet can help to reduce symptoms of kidney disease such as fatigue, swelling, and decreased appetite. This can make it easier to manage your condition and improve your overall quality of life.

A renal diet can be incredibly beneficial for those suffering from kidney disease. It can help to keep your blood pressure and cholesterol in check, as well as aiding in weight loss and reducing symptoms of kidney disease. If you are living with kidney disease, following a renal diet can be greatly beneficial for your health and well being.

CHAPTER 3:
MINERALS IN RENAL DIET

Minerals are essential components of a healthy diet, and they play an especially important role in a renal diet. Minerals like calcium, phosphorus, potassium, and sodium are all important for maintaining the proper balance of electrolytes and fluids in the body. However, for those with kidney disease, it is important to pay special attention to the intake of these minerals and to adjust the levels accordingly.

Calcium is an important mineral for maintaining healthy bones and teeth, and it is also important for blood clotting. For those with kidney disease, it is important to consume the recommended daily allowance (RDA) of calcium, which is 1000mg for adults. However, those with kidney disease should also be aware that too much calcium can lead to an increased risk of kidney stones.

Phosphorus is another important mineral for a renal diet. It is important for bone health and also helps regulate the acid base balance in the body. The RDA for phosphorus is 700mg for adults, but those with kidney disease should be careful not to consume too much as it can lead to an increase in phosphorus levels in the blood, which can cause serious complications.

Potassium is essential for maintaining healthy nerve and muscle function, and it also helps regulate the body's water and acid base balance. The RDA for potassium is 4.7g for adults, but those with kidney disease should be careful not to consume too much as it can lead to an increase in potassium levels in the blood, which can be dangerous.

Sodium is important for maintaining the body's fluid balance, and it is also involved in nerve and muscle function. The RDA for sodium is 2.3g for adults, but those with kidney disease should be careful not to consume too much as it can lead to an increase in sodium levels in the blood, which can cause serious health complications.

In conclusion, minerals are an important part of a healthy diet, but those with kidney disease should pay special attention to the intake of these minerals and adjust the levels accordingly to avoid any potential complications. By following a renal diet, you can ensure that you are getting the right amount of minerals to keep your body healthy and functioning properly.

BREAKFAST RECIPES:

OATMEAL WITH APPLES AND WALNUTS

Time to Prepare: 10 minutes | Servings: 2 | Cooking Time: 5 minutes

Ingredients:

- ½ cup rolled oats
- 1 cup nonfat milk
- 2 tablespoons honey
- 2 teaspoons ground cinnamon
- ½ cup diced apples
- 2 tablespoons chopped walnuts

Directions:

1. In a small saucepan, combine the oats, milk, honey, and cinnamon.
2. Bring to a low simmer, stirring occasionally.
3. Simmer for 5 minutes, stirring occasionally.
4. Divide the oatmeal into two bowls and top with apples and walnuts.

Nutritional Information: Calories: 245; Fat: 5g; Protein: 8g; Carbs: 45g; Sodium: 120mg; Fiber: 5g

EGG AND SALSA BREAKFAST WRAP

Time to Prepare: 10 minutes | Servings: 1 | Cooking Time: 5 minutes

Ingredients:

- 1 whole wheat tortilla
- 1 tablespoon salsa
- 2 eggs, lightly beaten
- 1 tablespoon shredded cheese
- 1 tablespoon diced onion
- Salt and pepper to taste

Directions:

1. Heat a nonstick skillet over medium high heat.
2. Place the tortilla in the skillet and cook until lightly toasted, about 1 minute each side.
3. Reduce the heat to medium low and add the salsa to the tortilla.
4. Pour the eggs over the salsa and scramble until cooked through.
5. Top the eggs with cheese and onion, and season with salt and pepper to taste.
6. Roll up the wrap and serve.

Nutritional Information: Calories: 264; Fat: 11g; Protein: 15g; Carbs: 25g; Sodium: 525mg; Fiber: 4g

BAKED OMELET

Time to Prepare: 10 minutes | Servings: 2 | Cooking Time: 20 minutes

Ingredients:

- 2 tablespoons olive oil
- 1 small onion, diced
- 1 bell pepper, diced
- 2 cloves garlic, minced
- 1 cup mushrooms, diced
- 4 eggs
- ½ cup nonfat milk
- ½ cup shredded cheese
- Salt and pepper to taste

Directions:

1. Preheat the oven to 375°F.
2. In a medium skillet, heat the olive oil over medium heat.
3. Add the onion, bell pepper, garlic, and mushrooms, and cook until softened, about 5 minutes.
4. In a medium bowl, whisk together the eggs and milk.
5. Pour the egg mixture into a 9 inch baking dish and top with the vegetables.
6. Sprinkle with the cheese and season with salt and pepper.
7. Bake for 20 minutes, or until the eggs are set.

Nutritional Information: Calories: 216; Fat: 14g; Protein: 14g; Carbs: 8g; Sodium: 264mg; Fiber: 2g

---

EGG AND BROCCOLI SKILLET

Time to Prepare: 10 minutes | Servings: 2 | Cooking Time: 8 minutes

Ingredients:

- 2 tablespoons olive oil
- ½ cup diced onion
- 2 cloves garlic, minced
- 2 cups broccoli florets
- 4 eggs
- Salt and pepper to taste

Directions:

1. Heat the olive oil in a large skillet over medium high heat.
2. Add the onion and garlic and cook until softened, about 3 minutes.
3. Add the broccoli and cook until tender, about 5 minutes.
4. Crack the eggs into the skillet and scramble until cooked through.
5. Season with salt and pepper to taste.

Nutritional Information: Calories: 214; Fat: 14g; Protein: 13g; Carbs: 8g; Sodium: 270mg; Fiber: 3g

BAKED EGGS WITH SPINACH

Time to Prepare: 10 minutes | Servings: 2 | Cooking Time: 15 minutes

Ingredients:

- 2 tablespoons olive oil
- ½ cup diced onion
- 2 cloves garlic, minced
- 2 cups baby spinach
- 4 eggs
- Salt and pepper to taste

Directions:

1. Preheat the oven to 375°F.
2. Heat the olive oil in a large skillet over medium high heat.
3. Add the onion and garlic and cook until softened, about 3 minutes.
4. Add the spinach and cook until wilted, about 2 minutes.
5. Divide the spinach mixture between two oven safe dishes.
6. Crack an egg into each dish and season with salt and pepper to taste.
7. Bake for 15 minutes, or until the eggs are set.

Nutritional Information: Calories: 199; Fat: 13g; Protein: 12g; Carbs: 8g; Sodium: 240mg; Fiber: 2g

---

VEGGIE FRITTATA

Time to Prepare: 10 minutes | Servings: 4 | Cooking Time: 20 minutes

Ingredients:

- 2 tablespoons olive oil
- ½ cup diced onion
- 2 cloves garlic, minced
- 1 cup diced bell pepper
- ½ cup diced mushrooms
- ½ cup diced tomatoes
- 8 eggs
- Salt and pepper to taste

Directions:

1. Preheat the oven to 375°F.
2. Heat the olive oil in a large skillet over medium high heat.
3. Add the onion and garlic and cook until softened, about 3 minutes.
4. Add the bell pepper, mushrooms, and tomatoes and cook until softened, about 5 minutes.
5. In a medium bowl, whisk together the eggs.
6. Pour the egg mixture into the skillet and season with salt and pepper.
7. Stir to combine and cook until the eggs are just set, about 5 minutes.
8. Transfer the skillet to the oven and bake for 10 minutes, or until the eggs are set.

Nutritional Information: Calories: 202; Fat: 13g; Protein: 13g; Carbs: 7g; Sodium: 285mg; Fiber: 2g

SWEET POTATO HASH

Time to Prepare: 10 minutes | Servings: 4 | Cooking Time: 15 minutes

Ingredients:

- 2 tablespoons olive oil
- 2 small sweet potatoes, diced
- 1 cup diced onion
- 1 cup diced bell pepper
- 1 cup diced mushrooms
- 4 eggs
- Salt and pepper to taste

Directions:

1. Heat the olive oil in a large skillet over medium high heat.
2. Add the sweet potatoes, onion, bell pepper, and mushrooms, and cook until softened, about 8 minutes.
3. Crack the eggs into the skillet and scramble until cooked through.
4. Season with salt and pepper to taste.

Nutritional Information: Calories: 197; Fat: 12g; Protein: 10g; Carbs: 12g; Sodium: 240mg; Fiber: 3g

---

AVOCADO TOAST WITH EGG

Time to Prepare: 10 minutes | Servings: 1 | Cooking Time: 5 minutes

Ingredients:

- 1 slice whole wheat bread
- 1 teaspoon olive oil
- 1 egg
- ½ avocado, mashed
- Salt and pepper to taste

Directions:

1. Heat a nonstick skillet over medium high heat.
2. Add the olive oil to the skillet and swirl to coat.
3. Crack the egg into the skillet and cook until the whites are set, about 2 minutes.
4. Meanwhile, toast the bread.
5. When the egg is cooked, transfer to the toast and top with the mashed avocado.
6. Season with salt and pepper to taste.

Nutritional Information: Calories: 286; Fat: 19g; Protein: 12g; Carbs: 20g; Sodium: 172mg; Fiber: 6g

FRUIT AND YOGURT PARFAIT

Time to Prepare: 10 minutes | Servings: 1 | Cooking Time: 0 minutes

Ingredients:

- ½ cup plain nonfat yogurt
- ½ cup diced fresh fruit (such as strawberries, blueberries, or raspberries)
- 1 tablespoon honey
- 2 tablespoons chopped walnuts

Directions:

1. In a small bowl, combine the yogurt and honey.
2. Layer the yogurt in a tall glass with the diced fruit.
3. Top with the chopped walnuts.

Nutritional Information: Calories: 280; Fat: 10g; Protein: 9g; Carbs: 39g; Sodium: 80mg; Fiber: 3g

---

COTTAGE CHEESE PANCAKES

Time to Prepare: 10 minutes | Servings: 2 | Cooking Time: 10 minutes

Ingredients:

- ½ cup nonfat cottage cheese
- 2 eggs
- 1 tablespoon almond flour
- 2 tablespoons honey
- 1 teaspoon ground cinnamon
- 2 tablespoons chopped walnuts
- 2 tablespoons butter

Directions:

1. In a medium bowl, whisk together the cottage cheese, eggs, almond flour, honey, and cinnamon.
2. Heat a nonstick skillet over medium heat.
3. Add the butter to the skillet and swirl to coat.
4. Pour the batter into the skillet, using a ¼ cup measure.
5. Cook for 4 minutes, or until the edges are golden.
6. Flip and cook for an additional 4 minutes, or until the pancakes are cooked through.
7. Top with walnuts and serve.

Nutritional Information: Calories: 361; Fat: 19g; Protein: 18g; Carbs: 33g; Sodium: 343mg; Fiber: 2g

BANANA SMOOTHIE

Time to Prepare: 5 minutes | Servings: 1 | Cooking Time: 0 minutes

Ingredients:

- 1 banana
- ½ cup nonfat milk
- ½ cup plain nonfat yogurt
- ¼ teaspoon ground cinnamon
- 2 tablespoons honey

Directions:

1. Place all ingredients in a blender and blend until smooth.
2. Pour into a glass and serve.

Nutritional Information: Calories: 253; Fat: 2g; Protein: 8g; Carbs: 52g; Sodium: 135mg; Fiber: 3g

EGG AND POTATO BREAKFAST BOWL

Time to Prepare: 10 minutes | Servings: 2 | Cooking Time: 20 minutes

Ingredients:

- 2 tablespoons olive oil
- 2 small potatoes, diced
- ½ cup diced onion
- 2 cloves garlic, minced
- 4 eggs
- Salt and pepper to taste

Directions:

1. Preheat the oven to 375°F.
2. Heat the olive oil in a medium skillet over medium high heat.
3. Add the potatoes, onion, and garlic, and cook until softened, about 8 minutes.
4. Meanwhile, crack the eggs into a small bowl and whisk together.
5. Add the eggs to the skillet and scramble until cooked through.
6. Transfer the skillet to the oven and bake for 10 minutes, or until the eggs are set.
7. Season with salt and pepper to taste.

Nutritional Information: Calories: 234; Fat: 15g; Protein: 11g; Carbs: 13g; Sodium: 242mg; Fiber: 2g

BREAKFAST BURRITO

Time to Prepare: 10 minutes | Servings: 1 | Cooking Time: 5 minutes

Ingredients:

- 1 whole wheat tortilla
- 2 eggs, lightly beaten
- 2 tablespoons salsa
- 2 tablespoons shredded cheese
- 1 tablespoon diced onion
- Salt and pepper to taste

Directions:

1. Heat a nonstick skillet over medium high heat.
2. Place the tortilla in the skillet and cook until lightly toasted, about 1 minute each side.
3. Reduce the heat to medium low and add the salsa to the tortilla.
4. Pour the eggs over the salsa and scramble until cooked through.
5. Top the eggs with cheese and onion, and season with salt and pepper to taste.
6. Roll up the burrito and serve.

Nutritional Information: Calories: 285; Fat: 14g; Protein: 15g; Carbs: 24g; Sodium: 518mg; Fiber: 4g

---

BREAKFAST TACOS

Time to Prepare: 10 minutes | Servings: 2 | Cooking Time: 5 minutes

Ingredients:

- 2 tablespoons olive oil
- ½ cup diced onion
- 2 cloves garlic, minced
- 2 cups baby spinach
- 4 eggs
- 4 corn tortillas
- 2 tablespoons salsa
- 2 tablespoons shredded cheese
- Salt and pepper to taste

Directions:

1. Heat the olive oil in a large skillet over medium high heat.
2. Add the onion and garlic and cook until softened, about 3 minutes.
3. Add the spinach and cook until wilted, about 2 minutes.
4. Crack the eggs into the skillet and scramble until cooked through.
5. Spoon the egg mixture onto the tortillas and top with salsa and cheese.
6. Season with salt and pepper to taste.

Nutritional Information: Calories: 288; Fat: 17g; Protein: 14g; Carbs: 20g; Sodium: 348mg; Fiber: 4g

BREAKFAST SANDWICH

Time to Prepare: 10 minutes | Servings: 1 | Cooking Time: 5 minutes

Ingredients:

- 2 slices whole wheat bread
- 1 tablespoon butter
- 1 egg
- 2 slices tomato
- 2 slices cooked bacon
- 1 tablespoon shredded cheese
- Salt and pepper to taste

Directions:

1. Heat a nonstick skillet over medium high heat.
2. Spread the butter on one side of each slice of bread.
3. Place one slice of bread, butter side down, in the skillet.
4. Crack the egg into the skillet and cook until the whites are set, about 2 minutes.
5. Top the egg with the tomato, bacon, and cheese.
6. Place the other slice of bread, butter side up, on top and cook until golden, about 2 minutes.
7. Season with salt and pepper to taste.

Nutritional Information: Calories: 398; Fat: 23g; Protein: 16g; Carbs: 32g; Sodium: 573mg; Fiber: 4g

LUNCH RECIPES:

GRILLED SALMON WITH ASPARAGUS AND WILD RICE

Time to Prepare: 10 minutes | Servings: 2 | Cooking time: 20 minutes

Ingredients:

- 2 salmon fillets
- 4 ounces asparagus
- 1 cup cooked wild rice
- 2 tablespoons olive oil
- Salt and pepper to taste
- 2 tablespoons fresh lemon juice

Directions:

1. Preheat oven to 375 degrees F.
2. Place salmon fillets on a baking sheet and brush with olive oil.
3. Season with salt and pepper.
4. Bake for 20 minutes until salmon is cooked through.
5. Meanwhile, in a large skillet, heat remaining olive oil over medium high heat.
6. Add asparagus and sauté for 5 minutes.
7. Add cooked wild rice and stir to combine.
8. Reduce heat to medium low and simmer for 5 minutes.
9. Serve salmon with asparagus and wild rice, and top with fresh lemon juice.

Nutritional Information: Calories: 327: Total Fat: 12.9g : Saturated Fat: 2.1g: Cholesterol: 45mg: Sodium: 104mg: Carbohydrates: 20.1g: Fiber: 3.3g: Protein: 27.3g

---

BROCCOLI AND CHEESE STUFFED BAKED POTATOES

Time to Prepare: 10 minutes | Servings: 4 | Cooking time: 40 minutes

Ingredients:

- 4 large baking potatoes
- 1/2 cup shredded cheddar cheese
- 1/2 cup cooked broccoli florets
- 2 tablespoons butter
- 2 tablespoons chopped green onion
- Salt and pepper to taste

Directions:

1. Preheat oven to 375 degrees F.
2. Wash potatoes and pierce several times with a fork.
3. Bake potatoes for 40 minutes until tender.
4. Cut potatoes in half and scoop out the insides, leaving a thin shell.
5. In a medium bowl, mix together potato insides, cheese, broccoli, butter, green onion, salt and pepper.
6. Stuff each potato shell with the potato mixture.
7. Place stuffed potatoes on a greased baking sheet and bake for 10 minutes.

Nutritional Information: Calories: 253: Total Fat: 8.9g: Saturated Fat: 5.2g: Cholesterol: 21mg: Sodium: 163mg: Carbohydrates: 36.4g: Fiber: 4.4g: Protein: 7.6g

COCONUT CURRY CHICKEN

Time to Prepare: 10 minutes | Servings: 4 | Cooking time: 20 minutes

Ingredients:

- 1 pound boneless, skinless chicken breasts, cut into small cubes
- 1 tablespoon olive oil
- 1 onion, diced
- 2 cloves garlic, minced
- 1 teaspoon ground ginger
- 1 teaspoon ground cumin
- 1 teaspoon ground turmeric
- 1/2 teaspoon ground coriander
- 1/2 teaspoon ground cinnamon
- 1/4 teaspoon cayenne pepper
- 1 can unsweetened coconut milk
- Salt and pepper to taste

Directions:

1. Heat olive oil in a large skillet over medium heat.
2. Add chicken and cook until lightly browned, about 5 minutes.
3. Add onion, garlic, ginger, cumin, turmeric, coriander, cinnamon and cayenne pepper. Cook for 5 minutes, stirring frequently.
4. Pour in coconut milk and bring to a simmer.
5. Simmer for 10 minutes, stirring occasionally, until chicken is cooked through and sauce has thickened.
6. Season with salt and pepper to taste.

Nutritional Information: Calories: 289: Total Fat: 16.3g: Saturated Fat: 11.3g: Cholesterol: 73mg: Sodium: 73mg: Carbohydrates: 7.6g: Fiber: 2.9g: Protein: 26.3g

---

SPINACH AND FETA FRITTATA

Time to Prepare: 10 minutes | Servings: 4 | Cooking time: 20 minutes

Ingredients:

- 2 tablespoons olive oil
- 1 onion, diced
- 2 cloves garlic, minced
- 6 eggs
- 1 cup cooked spinach
- 1/4 cup crumbled feta cheese
- Salt and pepper to taste

Directions:

1. Preheat oven to 350 degrees F.
2. Heat olive oil in an oven safe skillet over medium heat.
3. Add onion and garlic and cook for 5 minutes until softened.
4. In a medium bowl, whisk together eggs, spinach, feta cheese, salt and pepper.
5. Pour egg mixture into skillet and cook for 5 minutes, stirring occasionally until eggs are partially set.
6. Place skillet in preheated oven and bake for 10 minutes until eggs are completely set.

Nutritional Information: Calories: 200: Total Fat: 12.9g: Saturated Fat: 4.3g: Cholesterol: 210mg: Sodium: 256mg: Carbohydrates: 5.5g: Fiber: 1.5g: Protein: 13.5g

QUINOA AND BLACK BEAN SALAD

Time to Prepare: 10 minutes | Servings: 4 | Cooking time: 15 minutes

Ingredients:

- 1 cup uncooked quinoa
- 2 cups cooked black beans
- 1/2 cup diced red onion
- 1/2 cup diced red bell pepper
- 1/4 cup chopped fresh cilantro
- 2 tablespoons olive oil
- 2 tablespoons fresh lime juice
- Salt and pepper to taste

Directions:

1. Bring 2 cups of water to a boil in a medium saucepan.
2. Add quinoa and simmer for 15 minutes until quinoa is cooked and all liquid has been absorbed.
3. In a large bowl, combine cooked quinoa, black beans, onion, bell pepper and cilantro.
4. In a small bowl, whisk together olive oil and lime juice.
5. Pour over quinoa mixture and stir to combine.
6. Season with salt and pepper to taste.

Nutritional Information: Calories: 231: Total Fat: 6.7g: Saturated Fat: 1.0g: Cholesterol: 0mg: Sodium: 19mg: Carbohydrates: 34.3g: Fiber: 7.5g: Protein: 9.5g

---

ROASTED CAULIFLOWER SOUP

Time to Prepare: 10 minutes | Servings: 4 | Cooking time: 40 minutes

Ingredients:

- 2 heads cauliflower, cut into florets
- 2 tablespoons olive oil
- 2 cloves garlic, minced
- 4 cups vegetable broth
- 1/4 cup plain Greek yogurt
- 2 tablespoons fresh lemon juice
- Salt and pepper to taste

Directions:

1. Preheat oven to 400 degrees F.
2. Place cauliflower florets on a baking sheet and brush with olive oil.
3. Roast for 30 minutes until lightly browned.
4. Heat remaining olive oil in a large pot over medium heat.
5. Add garlic and cook for 1 minute until fragrant.
6. Add roasted cauliflower and vegetable broth and bring to a simmer.
7. Simmer for 10 minutes.
8. Remove from heat and blend with an immersion blender until smooth.
9. Stir in Greek yogurt and lemon juice.
10. Season with salt and pepper to taste.

Nutritional Information: Calories: 140: Total Fat: 7.1g: Saturated Fat: 1.1g: Cholesterol: 0mg: Sodium: 790mg: Carbohydrates: 15.3g: Fiber: 5.2g: Protein: 6.3g

BAKED COD WITH ROASTED VEGETABLES

Time to Prepare: 10 minutes | Servings: 4 | Cooking time: 30 minutes

Ingredients:

- 4 cod fillets
- 2 tablespoons olive oil
- 1 red bell pepper, chopped
- 1 yellow bell pepper, chopped
- 1 onion, chopped
- 1 zucchini, chopped
- 2 cloves garlic, minced
- Salt and pepper to taste

Directions:

1. Preheat oven to 375 degrees F.
2. Place cod fillets on a greased baking sheet and brush with olive oil.
3. Season with salt and pepper.
4. Bake for 20 minutes until cod is cooked through.
5. Meanwhile, in a large bowl, mix together bell peppers, onion, zucchini, garlic, remaining olive oil, salt and pepper.
6. Place vegetables on a baking sheet and roast for 10 minutes until tender.
7. Serve cod with roasted vegetables.

Nutritional Information: Calories: 244: Total Fat: 9.3g: Saturated Fat: 1.3g: Cholesterol: 42mg: Sodium: 84mg: Carbohydrates: 13.8g: Fiber: 4.2g: Protein: 25.3g

---

LENTIL AND TOMATO SOUP

Time to Prepare: 10 minutes | Servings: 4 | Cooking time: 30 minutes

Ingredients:

- 1 tablespoon olive oil
- 1 onion, diced
- 2 cloves garlic, minced
- 1 teaspoon dried oregano
- 1 teaspoon dried basil
- 1 can diced tomatoes
- 2 cups cooked lentils
- 4 cups vegetable broth
- Salt and pepper to taste

Directions:

1. Heat olive oil in a large pot over medium heat.
2. Add onion and garlic and cook for 5 minutes until softened.
3. Add oregano and basil and cook for 1 minute until fragrant.
4. Add diced tomatoes, lentils and vegetable broth and bring to a simmer.
5. Simmer for 20 minutes, stirring occasionally.
6. Season with salt and pepper to taste.

Nutritional Information: Calories: 213: Total Fat: 3.4g: Saturated Fat: 0.5g: Cholesterol: 0mg: Sodium: 664mg: Carbohydrates: 35.1g: Fiber: 11.2g: Protein: 12.9g

BAKED SALMON WITH MANGO SALSA

Time to Prepare: 10 minutes | Servings: 4 | Cooking time: 20 minutes

Ingredients:

- 4 salmon fillets
- 2 tablespoons olive oil
- 2 mangos, diced
- 1/2 red onion, diced
- 2 tablespoons chopped fresh cilantro
- 2 tablespoons fresh lime juice
- Salt and pepper to taste

Directions:

1. Preheat oven to 375 degrees F.
2. Place salmon fillets on a greased baking sheet and brush with olive oil.
3. Season with salt and pepper.
4. Bake for 20 minutes until salmon is cooked through.
5. Meanwhile, in a medium bowl, mix together mangos, onion, cilantro, lime juice, salt and pepper.
6. Serve salmon with mango salsa.

Nutritional Information: Calories: 267: Total Fat: 13.2g: Saturated Fat: 1.9g: Cholesterol: 45mg: Sodium: 83mg: Carbohydrates: 17.4g: Fiber: 3.2g: Protein: 22.2g

---

BAKED EGGPLANT PARMESAN

Time to Prepare: 10 minutes | Servings: 4 | Cooking time: 30 minutes

Ingredients:

- 2 large eggplants, sliced into 1/2 inch thick slices
- 2 tablespoons olive oil
- 1 cup marinara sauce
- 1 cup shredded mozzare-lla cheese
- 1/4 cup grated parmesan cheese
- Salt and pepper to taste

Directions:

1. Preheat oven to 375 degrees F.
2. Place eggplant slices on a greased baking sheet and brush with olive oil.
3. Season with salt and pepper.
4. Bake for 20 minutes until eggplant is tender.
5. Meanwhile, pour marinara sauce into a small baking dish.
6. Top with eggplant slices, mozzarella cheese and parmesan cheese.
7. Bake for 10 minutes until cheese is melted and bubbly.

Nutritional Information: Calories: 214: Total Fat: 12.4g: Saturated Fat: 3.8g: Cholesterol: 12mg: Sodium: 395mg: Carbohydrates: 15.9g: Fiber: 6.3g: Protein: 10.3g

STUFFED PEPPERS WITH LENTILS AND RICE

Time to Prepare: 10 minutes | Servings: 4 | Cooking time: 30 minutes

Ingredients:

- 4 bell peppers, halved and seeded
- 2 tablespoons olive oil
- 1 onion, diced
- 2 cloves garlic, minced
- 1 cup cooked lentils
- 1/2 cup cooked white rice
- 1/4 cup chopped fresh parsley
- Salt and pepper to taste

Directions:

1. Preheat oven to 375 degrees F.
2. Place bell pepper halves on a greased baking sheet.
3. Heat olive oil in a large skillet over medium heat.
4. Add onion and garlic and cook for 5 minutes until softened.
5. Add lentils, rice, parsley, salt and pepper and stir to combine.
6. Fill each pepper half with lentil mixture.
7. Bake for 25 minutes until peppers are tender.

Nutritional Information: Calories: 209: Total Fat: 7.7g: Saturated Fat: 1.1g: Cholesterol: 0mg: Sodium: 66mg: Carbohydrates: 29.3g: Fiber: 8.2g: Protein: 8.3g

LENTIL AND SPINACH SALAD

Time to Prepare: 10 minutes | Servings: 4 | Cooking time: 15 minutes

Ingredients:

- 1 cup uncooked lentils
- 2 tablespoons olive oil
- 2 cloves garlic, minced
- 2 cups cooked spinach
- 1/4 cup chopped fresh parsley
- 2 tablespoons fresh lemon juice
- Salt and pepper to taste

Directions:

1. Bring 2 cups of water to a boil in a medium saucepan.
2. Add lentils and simmer for 15 minutes until lentils are cooked and all liquid has been absorbed.
3. Heat olive oil in a large skillet over medium heat.
4. Add garlic and cook for 1 minute until fragrant.
5. Add cooked lentils and spinach and cook for 5 minutes, stirring frequently.
6. Remove from heat and stir in parsley and lemon juice.
7. Season with salt and pepper to taste.

Nutritional Information: Calories: 199: Total Fat: 6.5g: Saturated Fat: 0.9g: Cholesterol: 0mg: Sodium: 16mg: Carbohydrates: 28.7g: Fiber: 9.7g: Protein: 9.4g

GREEK SALAD WITH CHICKPEAS

Time to Prepare: 10 minutes | Servings: 4 | Cooking time: 0 minutes

Ingredients:

- 2 cups cooked chickpeas
- 1 cucumber, diced
- 1/2 red onion, diced
- 1/2 cup crumbled feta cheese
- 1/4 cup chopped fresh mint
- 2 tablespoons olive oil
- 2 tablespoons red wine vinegar
- Salt and pepper to taste

Directions:

1. In a large bowl, mix together chickpeas, cucumber, onion, feta cheese, and mint.
2. Whisk together olive oil and red wine vinegar in a small bowl.
3. Pour over the chickpea mixture and stir to combine.
4. Season with salt and pepper to taste.

Nutritional Information: Calories: 237: Total Fat: 11.3g: Saturated Fat: 3.2g: Cholesterol: 12mg: Sodium: 212mg: Carbohydrates: 25.1g: Fiber: 6.8g: Protein: 9.1g

---

BAKED ZUCCHINI FRITTERS

Time to Prepare: 10 minutes | Servings: 4 | Cooking time: 25 minutes

Ingredients:

- 2 zucchini, grated
- 2 tablespoons olive oil
- 1/4 cup all purpose flour
- 2 eggs, lightly beaten
- 1/4 cup grated parmesan cheese
- 2 tablespoons chopped fresh basil
- Salt and pepper to taste

Directions:

1. Preheat oven to 400 degrees F.
2. In a medium bowl, mix zucchini, olive oil, flour, eggs, parmesan cheese, basil, salt, and pepper.
3. Form mixture into 8 patties.
4. Place patties on a greased baking sheet and bake for 25 minutes until golden brown.

Nutritional Information: Calories: 209: Total Fat: 12.2g: Saturated Fat: 3.2g: Cholesterol: 86mg: Sodium: 206mg: Carbohydrates: 15.3g: Fiber: 2.3g: Protein: 9.5g

GRILLED VEGETABLE AND HALLOUMI SKEWERS

Time to Prepare: 10 minutes | Servings: 4 | Cooking time: 10 minutes

Ingredients:

- 1 red bell pepper, cut into 1 inch pieces
- 1 zucchini, cut into 1 inch pieces
- 1 eggplant, cut into 1 inch pieces
- 2 tablespoons olive oil
- 8 ounces halloumi cheese, cut into 1 inch cubes
- 2 tablespoons fresh lemon juice
- Salt and pepper to taste

Directions:

1. Preheat grill to medium high heat.
2. Mix bell pepper, zucchini, eggplant, olive oil, salt, and pepper in a large bowl.
3. Thread vegetables and halloumi onto skewers.
4. Grill for 10 minutes, occasionally turning, until vegetables are tender and halloumi is lightly browned.
5. Drizzle with lemon juice before serving.

Nutritional Information: Calories: 281: Total Fat: 19.3g: Saturated Fat: 10.9g: Cholesterol: 38mg: Sodium: 437mg: Carbohydrates: 13.2g: Fiber: 5.3g: Protein: 13.3g

DINNER RECIPES:

BAKED SALMON WITH ROASTED VEGETABLES

Time to prepare: 10 minutes | Servings: 4 | Cooking time: 30 minutes

Ingredients:

- 4 (4 oz) wild caught salmon fillets
- 2 medium sweet potatoes, peeled and diced
- 2 large carrots, peeled and diced
- 1 small onion, diced
- 2 tablespoons olive oil
- 2 tablespoons fresh lemon juice
- 2 tablespoons fresh parsley, minced
- 1 teaspoon garlic powder
- Salt and freshly ground black pepper, to taste

Directions:

1. Preheat the oven to 375°F.
2. Line a large baking sheet with parchment paper.
3. Place the salmon fillets onto the parchment lined baking sheet.
4. In a large bowl, combine the sweet potatoes, carrots, and onion together.
5. Drizzle the olive oil and lemon juice over the vegetables and toss to coat.
6. Spread the vegetables around the salmon fillets.
7. Sprinkle the parsley, garlic powder, salt, and pepper over the vegetables and salmon.
8. Bake for 25 30 minutes, or until the salmon is cooked through.
9. Serve immediately.

Nutritional Information: Calories: 239: Fat: 8.7 g: Protein: 21.7 g: Carbohydrates: 19.3 g: Sodium: 81 mg: Fiber: 3.1 g

---

GRILLED CHICKEN AND GREEN BEANS

Time to prepare: 10 minutes | Servings: 4 | Cooking time: 15 minutes

Ingredients:

- 4 (4 oz) boneless, skinless chicken breasts
- 1 tablespoon olive oil
- 2 cloves garlic, minced
- 2 tablespoons fresh thyme, minced
- 2 tablespoons fresh parsley, minced
- 2 cups fresh green beans, trimmed
- Salt and freshly ground black pepper, to taste

Directions:

1. Preheat a grill to medium high heat.
2. Rub the chicken breasts with the olive oil and season with garlic, thyme, parsley, salt, and pepper.
3. Place the chicken breasts on the hot grill and cook for about 7 minutes per side, or until cooked through.
4. Add the green beans to the hot grill and cook for 4 5 minutes, or until slightly charred and tender.
5. Serve the grilled chicken and green beans together.

Nutritional Information: Calories: 178: Fat: 5.7 g: Protein: 26.2 g: Carbohydrates: 6.2 g: Sodium: 130 mg: Fiber: 2.6 g

CHEESE AND SPINACH STUFFED SHELLS

Time to prepare: 10 minutes | Servings: 4 | Cooking time: 40 minutes

Ingredients:

- 12 jumbo shells
- 1 (15 oz) can low sodium tomato sauce
- 1 cup part skim ricotta cheese
- 1 cup frozen spinach, thawed and drained
- 1/2 cup shredded part skim mozzarella cheese
- 2 tablespoons grated Parmesan cheese
- 1 teaspoon garlic powder
- 1/2 teaspoon Italian seasoning
- Salt and freshly ground black pepper, to taste

Directions:

1. Preheat the oven to 350°F.
2. Grease a 9x13 inch baking dish with cooking spray.
3. Cook the jumbo shells according to package instructions.
4. In a large bowl, combine the tomato sauce, ricotta cheese, spinach, mozzarella cheese, Parmesan cheese, garlic powder, Italian seasoning, salt, and pepper.
5. Stuff each cooked jumbo shell with the cheese and spinach mixture.
6. Place the stuffed shells in the prepared baking dish.
7. Bake for 30 35 minutes, or until the cheese is melted and the shells are heated through.
8. Serve warm.

Nutritional Information: Calories: 271: Fat: 10.2 g: Protein: 18.7 g: Carbohydrates: 24.3 g: Sodium: 515 mg: Fiber: 3.2 g

BAKED HALIBUT WITH CREAMY LEMON SAUCE

Time to prepare: 10 minutes | Servings: 4 | Cooking time: 25 minutes

Ingredients:

- 4 (4 oz) halibut fillets
- 2 tablespoons olive oil
- 2 tablespoons fresh lemon juice
- 2 tablespoons fresh parsley, minced
- 2 cloves garlic, minced
- Salt and freshly ground black pepper, to taste
- 1/4 cup low sodium chicken broth
- 2 tablespoons unsalted butter
- 1/4 cup heavy cream

Directions:

1. Preheat the oven to 375°F.
2. Line a baking sheet with parchment paper.
3. Place the halibut fillets onto the parchment lined baking sheet.
4. Drizzle the olive oil and lemon juice over the halibut fillets.
5. Sprinkle the parsley, garlic, salt, and pepper over the fillets.
6. Bake for 20 25 minutes, or until the fish is cooked through.
7. Meanwhile, in a small saucepan over medium heat, combine the chicken broth, butter, and heavy cream.
8. Bring to a simmer and cook for 3 4 minutes, or until thickened.
9. Drizzle the creamy lemon sauce over the cooked halibut fillets and serve.

Nutritional Information: Calories: 285: Fat: 17.6 g: Protein: 26.5 g: Carbohydrates: 3.2 g: Sodium: 181 mg: Fiber: 0.2 g

---

BAKED TILAPIA WITH ROASTED TOMATOES

Time to prepare: 10 minutes | Servings: 4 | Cooking time: 25 minutes

Ingredients:

- 4 (4 oz) tilapia fillets
- 2 tablespoons olive oil
- 2 tablespoons fresh parsley, minced
- 2 cloves garlic, minced
- Salt and freshly ground black pepper, to taste
- 2 cups cherry tomatoes
- 2 tablespoons balsamic vinegar

Directions:

1. Preheat the oven to 375°F.
2. Line a baking sheet with parchment paper.
3. Place the tilapia fillets onto the parchment lined baking sheet.
4. Drizzle the olive oil over the tilapia fillets.
5. Sprinkle the parsley, garlic, salt, and pepper over the fillets.
6. Place the cherry tomatoes onto the baking sheet.
7. Drizzle the balsamic vinegar over the tomatoes.
8. Bake for 20 25 minutes, or until the tilapia is cooked through and the tomatoes are tender.
9. Serve warm.

Nutritional Information: Calories: 191: Fat: 8.2 g: Protein: 20.2 g: Carbohydrates: 6.9 g: Sodium: 79 mg: Fiber: 1.7 g

ROASTED VEGETABLE MEDLEY

Time to prepare: 10 minutes | Servings: 4 | Cooking time: 30 minutes

Ingredients:

- 2 large carrots, peeled and diced
- 2 medium sweet potatoes, peeled and diced
- 1 small onion, diced
- 1 large red bell pepper, diced
- 2 tablespoons olive oil
- 2 tablespoons fresh parsley, minced
- 1 teaspoon garlic powder
- Salt and freshly ground black pepper, to taste

Directions:

1. Preheat the oven to 375°F.
2. Line a large baking sheet with parchment paper.
3. Place the carrots, sweet potatoes, onion, and bell pepper onto the parchment lined baking sheet.
4. Drizzle the olive oil over the vegetables and toss to coat.
5. Sprinkle the parsley, garlic powder, salt, and pepper over the vegetables.
6. Roast for 25 30 minutes, or until the vegetables are tender.
7. Serve warm.

Nutritional Information: Calories: 137: Fat: 6.3 g: Protein: 2.5 g: Carbohydrates: 17.7 g: Sodium: 57 mg: Fiber: 4.4 g

---

ROASTED EGGPLANT AND CHICKPEAS

Time to prepare: 10 minutes | Servings: 4 | Cooking time: 40 minutes

Ingredients:

- 1 large eggplant, diced
- 1 (15 oz) can low sodium chickpeas, drained and rinsed
- 2 tablespoons olive oil
- 2 cloves garlic, minced
- 2 tablespoons fresh parsley, minced
- 2 tablespoons fresh oregano, minced
- Salt and freshly ground black pepper, to taste

Directions:

1. Preheat the oven to 375°F.
2. Line a large baking sheet with parchment paper.
3. Place the diced eggplant and chickpeas onto the parchment lined baking sheet.
4. Drizzle the olive oil over the eggplant and chickpeas and toss to coat.
5. Sprinkle the garlic, parsley, oregano, salt, and pepper over the vegetables.
6. Roast for 35 40 minutes, or until the vegetables are tender.
7. Serve warm.

Nutritional Information: Calories: 176: Fat: 7.7 g: Protein: 6.1 g: Carbohydrates: 21.6 g: Sodium: 123 mg: Fiber: 6.3 g

GRILLED ZUCCHINI AND MUSHROOMS

Time to prepare: 10 minutes | Servings: 4 | Cooking time: 10 minutes

Ingredients:

- 2 large zucchini, sliced
- 8 ounces mushrooms, sliced
- 2 tablespoons olive oil
- 2 cloves garlic, minced
- 2 tablespoons fresh thyme, minced
- Salt and freshly ground black pepper, to taste

Directions:

1. Preheat a grill to medium high heat.
2. Place the zucchini and mushrooms onto a large plate.
3. Drizzle the olive oil over the vegetables and toss to coat.
4. Sprinkle the garlic, thyme, salt, and pepper over the vegetables.
5. Place the vegetables onto the hot grill and cook for 5 7 minutes, or until tender.
6. Serve warm.

Nutritional Information: Calories: 119: Fat: 6.5 g: Protein: 4.3 g: Carbohydrates: 11.3 g: Sodium: 37 mg: Fiber: 3.0 g

---

LENTIL AND VEGETABLE STEW

Time to prepare: 10 minutes | Servings: 4 | Cooking time: 40 minutes

Ingredients:

- 2 tablespoons olive oil
- 2 cloves garlic, minced
- 1 large onion, diced
- 2 large carrots, peeled and diced
- 2 stalks celery, diced
- 2 cups low sodium vegetable broth
- 1 (15 oz) can low sodium diced tomatoes
- 1 cup dried green lentils, rinsed
- 2 tablespoons fresh parsley, minced
- 2 tablespoons fresh thyme, minced
- Salt and freshly ground black pepper, to taste

Directions:

1. Heat the olive oil in a large Dutch oven over medium heat.
2. Add the garlic, onion, carrots, and celery and cook for 5 minutes, or until the vegetables are softened.
3. Add the vegetable broth, tomatoes, lentils, parsley, thyme, salt, and pepper.
4. Bring to a boil, reduce the heat to low, and simmer for 30 35 minutes, or until the lentils are tender.
5. Serve warm.

Nutritional Information: Calories: 188: Fat: 4.3 g: Protein: 9.3 g: Carbohydrates: 28.3 g: Sodium: 225 mg: Fiber: 9.3 g

GRILLED VEGETABLE AND QUINOA SALAD

Time to prepare: 10 minutes | Servings: 4 | Cooking time: 30 minutes

Ingredients:

- 2 large zucchini, sliced
- 1 large eggplant, diced
- 8 ounces mushrooms, sliced
- 2 tablespoons olive oil
- 2 cloves garlic, minced
- 2 tablespoons fresh thyme, minced
- Salt and freshly ground black pepper, to taste
- 2 cups cooked quinoa
- 2 tablespoons fresh parsley, minced
- 2 tablespoons fresh lemon juice

Directions:

1. Preheat a grill to medium high heat.
2. Place the zucchini, eggplant, and mushrooms onto a large plate.
3. Drizzle the olive oil over the vegetables and toss to coat.
4. Sprinkle the garlic, thyme, salt, and pepper over the vegetables.
5. Place the vegetables onto the hot grill and cook for 5 7 minutes, or until tender.
6. In a large bowl, combine the cooked vegetables, quinoa, parsley, and lemon juice.
7. Toss to combine and season with additional salt and pepper, if desired.
8. Serve warm.

Nutritional Information: Calories: 242: Fat: 8.1 g: Protein: 8.3 g: Carbohydrates: 34.7 g: Sodium: 89 mg: Fiber: 7.2 g

---

BAKED SWEET POTATO FRIES

Time to prepare: 10 minutes | Servings: 4 | Cooking time: 25 minutes

Ingredients:

- 2 large sweet potatoes, peeled and cut into fries
- 2 tablespoons olive oil
- 2 tablespoons fresh parsley, minced
- 1 teaspoon garlic powder
- Salt and freshly ground black pepper, to taste

Directions:

1. Preheat the oven to 375°F.
2. Line a large baking sheet with parchment paper.
3. Place the sweet potato fries onto the parchment lined baking sheet.
4. Drizzle the olive oil over the fries and toss to coat.
5. Sprinkle the parsley, garlic powder, salt, and pepper over the fries.
6. Bake for 20 25 minutes, or until the fries are crispy.
7. Serve warm.

Nutritional Information: Calories: 150: Fat: 5.7 g: Protein: 2.6 g: Carbohydrates: 23.2 g: Sodium: 83 mg: Fiber: 3.4 g

BROILED TUNA PATTIES

Time to prepare: 10 minutes | Servings: 4 | Cooking time: 5 minutes

Ingredients:

- 1 (12 oz) can low sodium tuna, drained
- 1/4 cup bread crumbs
- 2 tablespoons olive oil
- 2 tablespoons fresh parsley, minced
- 1/2 teaspoon garlic powder
- 1 egg
- Salt and freshly ground black pepper, to taste

Directions:

1. Preheat the broiler to high heat.
2. Grease a large baking sheet with cooking spray.
3. In a large bowl, combine the tuna, bread crumbs, olive oil, parsley, garlic powder, egg, salt, and pepper.
4. Form the tuna mixture into 8 patties.
5. Place the patties onto the prepared baking sheet.
6. Broil for 3 4 minutes per side, or until the patties are crispy.
7. Serve warm.

Nutritional Information: Calories: 207: Fat: 8.7 g: Protein: 22.9 g: Carbohydrates: 7.2 g: Sodium: 145 mg: Fiber: 0.4 g

---

SLOW COOKER VEGGIE CHILI

Time to prepare: 10 minutes | Servings: 4 | Cooking time: 8 hours

Ingredients:

- 1 tablespoon olive oil
- 1 large onion, diced
- 2 cloves garlic, minced
- 2 large carrots, peeled and diced
- 2 stalks celery, diced
- 1 (15 oz) can low sodium diced tomatoes
- 1 (15 oz) can low sodium black beans, drained and rinsed
- 1 (15 oz) can low sodium kidney beans, drained and rinsed
- 1 (15 oz) can low sodium corn, drained
- 2 cups low sodium vegetable broth
- 2 tablespoons chili powder
- 2 teaspoons ground cumin
- Salt and freshly ground black pepper, to taste

Directions:

1. Heat the olive oil in a large skillet over medium heat.
2. Add the onion, garlic, carrots, and celery and cook for 5 minutes, or until the vegetables are softened.
3. Transfer the cooked vegetables to a slow cooker and add the diced tomatoes, black beans, kidney beans, corn, vegetable broth, chili powder, and cumin.
4. Stir to combine and season with salt and pepper.
5. Cover and cook on low heat for 8 hours or on high heat for 4 hours.
6. Serve warm with your favorite toppings.

Nutrition Information: Calories: 247: Fat: 3g: Carbohydrates: 44g: Protein: 11g: Fiber: 11g

SNACK AND SIDES RECIPES:

BAKED KALE CHIPS

Time to Prepare: 10 minutes | Servings: 4 | Cooking Time: 10 minutes

Ingredients:

- 2 bunches of kale, stems removed and chopped into pieces
- 1 tablespoon of olive oil
- 1 teaspoon of garlic powder
- 1 teaspoon of sea salt
- 1 teaspoon of black pepper

Directions:

1. Preheat oven to 350F. Line baking sheet with parchment paper.
2. In a large bowl, mix together chopped kale, olive oil, garlic powder, sea salt, and black pepper.
3. Spread kale mixture evenly on the baking sheet.
4. Bake for 10 minutes, or until the kale chips are golden and crispy.

Nutritional Information (per serving): Calories: 44: Fat: 2.7g: Carbohydrates: 3.9g: Protein: 1.4g

---

HUMMUS AND VEGGIE STICKS

Time to Prepare: 10 minutes | Servings: 4 | Cooking Time: 0 minutes

Ingredients:

- 2 cups of cooked chickpeas
- 1/4 cup of tahini
- 1/4 cup of fresh lemon juice
- 2 cloves of garlic
- 2 tablespoons of olive oil
- 1/2 teaspoon of sea salt
- 1/4 teaspoon of cumin
- 1/4 teaspoon of black pepper
- 1 cup of cut vegetables of your choice (carrots, cucumbers, celery, etc.)

Directions:

1. Combine chickpeas, tahini, lemon juice, garlic, olive oil, sea salt, cumin, and black pepper in a food processor or blender. Blend until smooth.
2. Serve hummus in a bowl with vegetables of your choice for dipping.

Nutritional Information (per serving): Calories: 190: Fat: 9.7g: Carbohydrates: 19.3g: Protein: 7.3g

BAKED SWEET POTATO FRIES

Time to Prepare: 10 minutes | Servings: 4 | Cooking Time: 25 minutes

Ingredients:

- 4 sweet potatoes, peeled and cut into fries
- 2 tablespoons of olive oil
- 1 teaspoon of garlic powder
- 1 teaspoon of sea salt
- 1 teaspoon of black pepper

Directions:

1. Preheat oven to 400F. Line baking sheet with parchment paper.
2. In a large bowl, combine sweet potato fries, olive oil, garlic powder, sea salt, and black pepper.
3. Spread fries evenly on the baking sheet.
4. Bake for 25 minutes, or until golden and crispy.

Nutritional Information (per serving): Calories: 173: Fat: 8.7g: Carbohydrates: 22.2g: Protein: 2.4g

---

BAKED ZUCCHINI FRITTERS

Time to Prepare: 10 minutes | Servings: 4 | Cooking Time: 25 minutes

Ingredients:

- 2 large zucchinis, grated
- 2 tablespoons of olive oil
- 2 tablespoons of almond flour
- 1 teaspoon of garlic powder
- 1 teaspoon of sea salt
- 1 teaspoon of black pepper
- 1/4 cup of chopped parsley

Directions:

1. Preheat oven to 400F. Line baking sheet with parchment paper.
2. In a large bowl, combine grated zucchini, olive oil, almond flour, garlic powder, sea salt, black pepper, and parsley.
3. Mix together until combined.
4. Form mixture into 4 patties and place on baking sheet.
5. Bake for 25 minutes, or until golden and crispy.

Nutritional Information (per serving): Calories: 118: Fat: 7.5g: Carbohydrates: 9.2g: Protein: 3.5g

QUINOA AND BLACK BEAN SALAD

Time to Prepare: 10 minutes | Servings: 4 | Cooking Time: 20 minutes

Ingredients:

- 1 cup of quinoa, cooked
- 1 cup of black beans, cooked
- 1/2 cup of diced red bell pepper
- 1/2 cup of diced red onion
- 1/4 cup of fresh lime juice
- 1/4 cup of olive oil
- 1/2 teaspoon of sea salt
- 1/4 teaspoon of black pepper
- 1/4 cup of chopped cilantro

Directions:

1. In a large bowl, combine cooked quinoa, cooked black beans, diced red bell pepper, diced red onion, fresh lime juice, olive oil, sea salt, and black pepper.
2. Mix together until combined.
3. Stir in chopped cilantro.
4. Serve chilled or at room temperature.

Nutritional Information (per serving): Calories: 286: Fat: 13.4g: Carbohydrates: 32.4g: Protein: 9.4g

ROASTED BRUSSELS SPROUTS

Time to Prepare: 10 minutes | Servings: 4 | Cooking Time: 25 minutes

Ingredients:

- 2 pounds of Brussels sprouts, halved
- 2 tablespoons of olive oil
- 1 teaspoon of garlic powder
- 1 teaspoon of sea salt
- 1 teaspoon of black pepper

Directions:

1. Preheat oven to 400F. Line baking sheet with parchment paper.
2. In a large bowl, combine Brussels sprouts, olive oil, garlic powder, sea salt, and black pepper.
3. Spread the Brussels sprouts evenly onto the baking sheet.
4. Bake for 25 minutes, or until golden and crispy.

Nutritional Information (per serving): Calories: 153: Fat: 7.5g: Carbohydrates: 16.1g: Protein: 6.5g

BROCCOLI AND AVOCADO SALAD

Time to Prepare: 10 minutes | Servings: 4 | Cooking Time: 0 minutes

Ingredients:

- 4 cups of broccoli florets
- 1 large avocado, diced
- 1/4 cup of sliced almonds
- 1/4 cup of chopped red onion
- 2 tablespoons of olive oil
- 2 tablespoons of fresh lemon juice
- 1 teaspoon of sea salt
- 1/4 teaspoon of black pepper

Directions:

1. In a large bowl, combine broccoli florets, avocado, sliced almonds, and chopped red onion.
2. In a small bowl, whisk together olive oil, lemon juice, sea salt, and black pepper.
3. Pour dressing over salad and mix together until combined.
4. Serve chilled or at room temperature.

Nutritional Information (per serving): Calories: 189: Fat: 14.3g: Carbohydrates: 12.3g: Protein: 5.1g

---

CUCUMBER AND RADISH SALAD

Time to Prepare: 10 minutes | Servings: 4 | Cooking Time: 0 minutes

Ingredients:

- 2 large cucumbers, diced
- 4 radishes, diced
- 1/4 cup of chopped parsley
- 2 tablespoons of olive oil
- 1 tablespoon of fresh lemon juice
- 1 teaspoon of sea salt
- 1/4 teaspoon of black pepper

Directions:

1. In a large bowl, combine diced cucumbers, diced radishes, and chopped parsley.
2. In a small bowl, whisk together olive oil, lemon juice, sea salt, and black pepper.
3. Pour dressing over salad and mix together until combined.
4. Serve chilled or at room temperature.

Nutritional Information (per serving): Calories: 104: Fat: 7.3g: Carbohydrates: 7.1g: Protein: 1.8g

BAKED SWEET POTATO WEDGES

Time to Prepare: 10 minutes | Servings: 4 | Cooking Time: 25 minutes

Ingredients:

- 4 sweet potatoes, cut into wedges
- 2 tablespoons of olive oil
- 1 teaspoon of garlic powder
- 1 teaspoon of sea salt
- 1 teaspoon of black pepper

Directions:

1. Preheat oven to 400F. Line baking sheet with parchment paper.
2. In a large bowl, combine sweet potato wedges, olive oil, garlic powder, sea salt, and black pepper.
3. Spread the wedges evenly onto the baking sheet.
4. Bake for 25 minutes, or until golden and crispy.

Nutritional Information (per serving): Calories: 173: Fat: 8.7g: Carbohydrates: 22.2g: Protein: 2.4g

BAKED APPLES

Time to Prepare: 10 minutes | Servings: 4 | Cooking Time: 25 minutes

Ingredients:

- 4 apples, cored and sliced
- 2 tablespoons of almond butter
- 1 teaspoon of ground cinnamon
- 1 teaspoon of sea salt
- 1/4 teaspoon of black pepper

Directions:

1. Preheat oven to 400F. Line baking sheet with parchment paper.
2. In a small bowl, mix together almond butter, ground cinnamon, sea salt, and black pepper.
3. Spread the almond butter mixture onto the apples slices.
4. Arrange the apples slices on the baking sheet.
5. Bake for 25 minutes, or until apples are tender.

Nutritional Information (per serving): Calories: 126: Fat: 6.2g: Carbohydrates: 16.6g: Protein: 2.1g

BAKED BUTTERNUT SQUASH

Time to Prepare: 10 minutes | Servings: 4 | Cooking Time: 25 minutes

Ingredients:

- 1 large butternut squash, peeled and cubed
- 2 tablespoons of olive oil
- 1 teaspoon of garlic powder
- 1 teaspoon of sea salt
- 1 teaspoon of black pepper

Directions:

1. Preheat oven to 400F. Line baking sheet with parchment paper.
2. In a large bowl, combine butternut squash, olive oil, garlic powder, sea salt, and black pepper.
3. Spread the squash cubes evenly onto the baking sheet.
4. Bake for 25 minutes, or until golden and crispy.

Nutritional Information (per serving): Calories: 166: Fat: 8.1g: Carbohydrates: 21.7g: Protein: 2.7g

---

BAKED EGGPLANT FRIES

Time to Prepare: 10 minutes | Servings: 4 | Cooking Time: 25 minutes

Ingredients:

- 1 large eggplant, cut into fries
- 2 tablespoons of olive oil
- 1 teaspoon of garlic powder
- 1 teaspoon of sea salt
- 1 teaspoon of black pepper

Directions:

1. Preheat oven to 400F. Line baking sheet with parchment paper.
2. In a large bowl, combine eggplant fries, olive oil, garlic powder, sea salt, and black pepper.
3. Spread the fries evenly onto the baking sheet.
4. Bake for 25 minutes, or until golden and crispy.

Nutritional Information (per serving): Calories: 150: Fat: 8.5g: Carbohydrates: 17.2g: Protein: 2.4g

AVOCADO TOAST

Time to Prepare: 10 minutes | Servings: 4 | Cooking Time: 0 minutes

Ingredients:

- 4 slices of whole grain bread
- 2 avocados, mashed
- 1/4 cup of chopped parsley
- 2 tablespoons of olive oil
- 2 tablespoons of fresh lemon juice
- 1 teaspoon of sea salt
- 1/4 teaspoon of black pepper

Directions:

1. Spread mashed avocado onto the slices of bread.
2. Sprinkle with chopped parsley.
3. In a small bowl, whisk together olive oil, lemon juice, sea salt, and black pepper.
4. Drizzle dressing over avocado toast and serve.

Nutritional Information (per serving): Calories: 282: Fat: 16.8g: Carbohydrates: 28.1g: Protein: 6.2g

BAKED TOFU FRIES

Time to Prepare: 10 minutes | Servings: 4 | Cooking Time: 25 minutes

Ingredients:

- 2 blocks of firm tofu, cut into fries
- 2 tablespoons of olive oil
- 1 teaspoon of garlic powder
- 1 teaspoon of sea salt
- 1 teaspoon of black pepper

Directions:

1. Preheat oven to 400F. Line baking sheet with parchment paper.
2. In a large bowl, combine tofu fries, olive oil, garlic powder, sea salt, and black pepper.
3. Spread the fries evenly onto the baking sheet.
4. Bake for 25 minutes, or until golden and crispy.

Nutritional Information (per serving): Calories: 191: Fat: 10.7g: Carbohydrates: 7.7g: Protein: 16.8g

BAKED FALAFEL

Time to Prepare: 10 minutes | Servings: 4 | Cooking Time: 25 minutes

Ingredients:

- 2 cups of cooked chickpeas
- 1/4 cup of chopped red onion
- 2 tablespoons of olive oil
- 1 teaspoon of garlic powder
- 1 teaspoon of sea salt
- 1 teaspoon of black pepper
- 1/4 cup of chopped parsley

Directions:

1. Preheat oven to 400F. Line baking sheet with parchment paper.
2. In a large bowl, combine cooked chickpeas, chopped red onion, olive oil, garlic powder, sea salt, black pepper, and chopped parsley.
3. Mix together until combined.
4. Form mixture into 4 patties and place on baking sheet.
5. Bake for 25 minutes, or until golden and crispy.

Nutritional Information (per serving): Calories: 187: Fat: 7.5g: Carbohydrates: 21.5g: Protein: 8.6g

DESSERT RECIPES:

MAPLE PECAN OATMEAL COOKIES

Time to Prepare: 10 minutes | Servings: 12 | Cooking Time: 12 minutes

Ingredients:

- 1 cup old fashioned oats
- 1/2 cup all purpose flour
- ¼ teaspoon baking powder
- ¼ teaspoon ground cinnamon
- ¼ teaspoon salt
- 1/3 cup butter, melted
- 1/4 cup maple syrup
- 1 large egg
- 1/3 cup chopped pecans

Directions:

1. Preheat oven to 350°F. Grease a baking sheet.
2. In a medium bowl, combine oats, flour, baking powder, cinnamon and salt.
3. In a small bowl, whisk together melted butter, maple syrup and egg.
4. Pour wet ingredients into dry ingredients and stir to combine. Stir in pecans.
5. Drop tablespoonfuls of dough onto prepared baking sheet. Bake for 12 minutes or until golden.

Nutritional Information: Calories: 89: Fat: 5g: Carbohydrates: 9g: Protein: 2g: Sodium: 68mg: Potassium: 18mg

BAKED APPLES

Time to Prepare: 5 minutes | Servings: 4 | Cooking Time: 15 minutes

Ingredients:

- 4 apples, cored and sliced
- 2 tablespoons honey
- 2 tablespoons brown sugar
- 1 teaspoon ground cinnamon
- ½ teaspoon ground nutmeg
- 2 tablespoons butter
- 2 tablespoons water

Directions:

1. Preheat oven to 375°F. Grease a baking dish.
2. Place apples in baking dish.
3. In a small bowl, combine honey, brown sugar, cinnamon, nutmeg and butter. Pour over apples.
4. Pour water into dish.
5. Bake for 15 minutes or until apples are tender.

Nutritional Information: Calories: 160: Fat: 7g: Carbohydrates: 27g: Protein: 1g: Sodium: 33mg: Potassium: 159mg

COCONUT LIME CUSTARD

Time to Prepare: 10 minutes | Servings: 4 | Cooking Time: 20 minutes

Ingredients:

- 1 can full fat coconut milk
- 2 large eggs
- 2 tablespoons honey
- 2 tablespoons lime juice
- 2 tablespoons cornstarch
- 1 teaspoon vanilla extract
- 1/4 teaspoon salt
- 1 tablespoon toasted coconut flakes

Directions:

1. Preheat oven to 350°F. Grease four ramekins.
2. In a medium bowl, whisk together coconut milk, eggs, honey, lime juice, cornstarch, vanilla and salt.
3. Divide mixture among ramekins and sprinkle with toasted coconut flakes.
4. Place ramekins in a baking dish and pour hot water into dish until it reaches halfway up the side of the ramekins.
5. Bake for 20 minutes or until custard is set.

Nutritional Information: Calories: 222: Fat: 15g: Carbohydrates: 20g: Protein: 6g: Sodium: 156mg: Potassium: 166mg

---

CARAMELIZED BANANA BREAD

Time to Prepare: 10 minutes | Servings: 10 | Cooking Time: 50 minutes

Ingredients:

- 1 cup all purpose flour
- 1 teaspoon baking powder
- 1 teaspoon ground cinnamon
- ¼ teaspoon salt
- 2 large bananas, mashed
- ½ cup brown sugar
- ¼ cup vegetable oil
- 2 tablespoons honey
- 2 large eggs
- 2 tablespoons toasted walnuts
- 2 tablespoons caramel sauce

Directions:

1. Preheat oven to 350°F. Grease a 9 inch loaf pan.
2. In a medium bowl, whisk together flour, baking powder, cinnamon and salt.
3. In a separate bowl, mix together mashed bananas, brown sugar, vegetable oil, honey and eggs.
4. Add wet ingredients to dry ingredients and mix until just combined.
5. Pour batter into prepared pan. Sprinkle with walnuts and drizzle with caramel sauce.
6. Bake for 50 minutes or until a toothpick inserted into the center comes out clean.

Nutritional Information: Calories: 201: Fat: 9g: Carbohydrates: 28g: Protein: 3g: Sodium: 106mg: Potassium: 156mg

APPLE CRANBERRY CRUMBLE

Time to Prepare: 10 minutes | Servings: 8 | Cooking Time: 35 minutes

Ingredients:

- 4 cups peeled, chopped apples
- 1 cup fresh cranberries
- 2 tablespoons honey
- 2 tablespoons brown sugar
- 2 tablespoons lemon juice
- 1 teaspoon ground cinnamon
- 1/2 cup all purpose flour
- 1/2 cup old fashioned oats
- 1/4 cup butter, melted

Directions:

1. Preheat oven to 350°F. Grease an 8 inch baking dish.
2. In a large bowl, combine apples, cranberries, honey, brown sugar, lemon juice and cinnamon. Pour into prepared baking dish.
3. In a medium bowl, mix together flour, oats and melted butter. Sprinkle over apple mixture.
4. Bake for 35 minutes or until apples are tender and topping is golden.

Nutritional Information: Calories: 186: Fat: 7g: Carbohydrates: 30g: Protein: 2g: Sodium: 31mg: Potassium: 120mg

---

CHOCOLATE CHIP OATMEAL COOKIES

Time to Prepare: 10 minutes | Servings: 12 | Cooking Time: 10 minutes

Ingredients:

- 1 cup old fashioned oats
- 1/2 cup all purpose flour
- 1/4 teaspoon baking powder
- 1/4 teaspoon baking soda
- 1/4 teaspoon salt
- 1/3 cup butter, melted
- 1/4 cup honey
- 1 large egg
- 1/2 cup semi sweet chocolate chips

Directions:

1. Preheat oven to 350°F. Grease a baking sheet.
2. In a medium bowl, combine oats, flour, baking powder, baking soda and salt.
3. In a small bowl, whisk together melted butter, honey and egg.
4. Pour wet ingredients into dry ingredients and stir to combine. Stir in chocolate chips.
5. Drop tablespoonfuls of dough onto prepared baking sheet. Bake for 10 minutes or until golden.

Nutritional Information: Calories: 130: Fat: 7g: Carbohydrates: 16g: Protein: 2g: Sodium: 78mg: Potassium: 58mg

BLUEBERRY YOGURT PARFAIT

Time to Prepare: 5 minutes | Servings: 2 | Cooking Time: 0 minutes

Ingredients:

- 2 cups plain Greek yogurt
- 1/2 cup fresh blueberries
- 2 tablespoons honey
- 2 tablespoons toasted coconut flakes

Directions:

1. In two glasses, layer yogurt and blueberries.
2. Drizzle each with honey and sprinkle with toasted coconut flakes.

Nutritional Information: Calories: 252: Fat: 6g: Carbohydrates: 33g: Protein: 17g:Sodium: 127mg: Potassium: 281mg

---

BAKED PEACHES

Time to Prepare: 5 minutes | Servings: 4 | Cooking Time: 15 minutes

Ingredients:

- 4 peaches, halved and pitted
- 2 tablespoons honey
- 2 tablespoons brown sugar
- 1 teaspoon ground cinnamon
- 2 tablespoons butter
- 2 tablespoons water

Directions:

1. Preheat oven to 375°F. Grease a baking dish.
2. Place peaches in baking dish.
3. In a small bowl, combine honey, brown sugar, cinnamon and butter. Pour over peaches.
4. Pour water into dish.
5. Bake for 15 minutes or until peaches are tender.

Nutritional Information: Calories: 116: Fat: 4g: Carbohydrates: 21g: Protein: 1g: Sodium: 33mg: Potassium: 243mg

VANILLA CUSTARD

Time to Prepare: 10 minutes | Servings: 4 | Cooking Time: 20 minutes

Ingredients:

- 2 cups half and half
- 2 large eggs
- 2 tablespoons honey
- 2 tablespoons cornstarch
- 1 teaspoon vanilla extract
- 1/4 teaspoon salt

Directions:

1. Preheat oven to 350°F. Grease four ramekins.
2. In a medium bowl, whisk together half and half, eggs, honey, cornstarch, vanilla and salt.
3. Divide mixture among ramekins.
4. Place ramekins in a baking dish and pour hot water into dish until it reaches halfway up the side of the ramekins.
5. Bake for 20 minutes or until custard is set.

Nutritional Information: Calories: 193: Fat: 11g: Carbohydrates: 18g: Protein: 6g: Sodium: 127mg: Potassium: 161mg

---

CHOCOLATE PUDDING

Time to Prepare: 5 minutes | Servings: 4 | Cooking Time: 0 minutes

Ingredients:

- 1 can full fat coconut milk
- 2 tablespoons honey
- 2 tablespoons cocoa powder
- 2 tablespoons cornstarch
- 1 teaspoon vanilla extract
- 1/4 teaspoon salt
- 2 tablespoons semi sweet chocolate chips

Directions:

1. In a medium bowl, whisk together coconut milk, honey, cocoa powder, cornstarch, vanilla and salt.
2. Divide mixture among four glasses. Sprinkle with chocolate chips.
3. Refrigerate for at least 1 hour before serving.

Nutritional Information: Calories: 175: Fat: 13g: Carbohydrates: 15g: Protein: 3g: Sodium: 79mg: Potassium: 152mg

BANANA COCONUT BREAD

Time to Prepare: 10 minutes | Servings: 10 | Cooking Time: 50 minutes

Ingredients:

- 1 cup all purpose flour
- 1 teaspoon baking powder
- 1 teaspoon ground cinnamon
- ¼ teaspoon salt
- 2 large bananas, mashed
- ½ cup brown sugar
- ¼ cup vegetable oil
- 2 tablespoons honey
- 2 large eggs
- 2 tablespoons toasted coconut flakes

Directions:

1. Preheat oven to 350°F. Grease a 9 inch loaf pan.
2. In a medium bowl, whisk together flour, baking powder, cinnamon and salt.
3. In a separate bowl, mix together mashed bananas, brown sugar, vegetable oil, honey and eggs.
4. Add wet ingredients to dry ingredients and mix until just combined.
5. Pour batter into prepared pan. Sprinkle with coconut flakes.
6. Bake for 50 minutes or until a toothpick inserted into the center comes out clean.

Nutritional Information: Calories: 201: Fat: 9g: Carbohydrates: 28g: Protein: 3g: Sodium: 107mg: Potassium: 156mg

NO BAKE COCONUT OATMEAL BARS

Time to Prepare: 10 minutes | Servings: 8 | Cooking Time: 0 minutes

Ingredients:

- 2 cups old fashioned oats
- 1/2 cup melted butter
- 1/4 cup honey
- 2 tablespoons brown sugar
- 1 teaspoon ground cinnamon
- 1/4 teaspoon salt
- 1/2 cup semi sweet chocolate chips
- 1/2 cup toasted coconut flakes

Directions:

1. Grease an 8 inch baking dish.
2. In a large bowl, mix together oats, melted butter, honey, brown sugar, cinnamon and salt.
3. Stir in chocolate chips and toasted coconut flakes.
4. Press mixture into prepared dish. Refrigerate for at least 1 hour before cutting into bars.

Nutritional Information: Calories: 262: Fat: 14g: Carbohydrates: 32g: Protein: 4g: Sodium: 122mg: Potassium: 97mg

BAKED APPLESAUCE

Time to Prepare: 10 minutes | Servings: 8 | Cooking Time: 30 minutes

Ingredients:

- 4 cups peeled, chopped apples
- 2 tablespoons honey
- 2 tablespoons brown sugar
- 1 teaspoon ground cinnamon
- 2 tablespoons butter
- 2 tablespoons water

Directions:

1. Preheat oven to 375°F. Grease an 8 inch baking dish.
2. In a large bowl, combine apples, honey, brown sugar and cinnamon. Pour into prepared baking dish.
3. Dot with butter and pour water into dish.
4. Bake for 30 minutes or until apples are tender.

Nutritional Information: Calories: 103: Fat: 3g: Carbohydrates: 20g: Protein: 0g: Sodium: 7mg: Potassium: 94mg

---

CHOCOLATE PEANUT BUTTER FUDGE

Time to Prepare: 10 minutes | Servings: 16 | Cooking Time: 0 minutes

Ingredients:

- 2 cups semi sweet chocolate chips
- ¼ cup creamy peanut butter
- 2 tablespoons honey
- 2 tablespoons butter
- 1 teaspoon vanilla extract
- 1/4 teaspoon salt

Directions:

1. Grease an 8 inch square baking dish.
2. In a medium saucepan, melt chocolate chips, peanut butter, honey, butter, vanilla and salt.
3. Pour mixture into prepared dish. Refrigerate for at least 1 hour before cutting into bars.

Nutritional Information: Calories: 175: Fat: 11g: Carbohydrates: 18g: Protein: 3g: Sodium: 99mg: Potassium: 99mg

CHOCOLATE COVERED STRAWBERRIES

Time to Prepare: 10 minutes | Servings: 8 | Cooking Time: 0 minutes

Ingredients:

- 2 cups semi sweet chocolate chips
- 1 tablespoon butter
- 2 tablespoons honey
- 8 large strawberries, washed and dried

Directions:

1. Place chocolate chips, butter and honey in a medium heat safe bowl.
2. Place bowl over a pot of simmering water, stirring until chocolate is melted and smooth.
3. Dip each strawberry into the melted chocolate, coating completely.
4. Place on a parchment lined baking sheet and refrigerate for at least 1 hour before serving.

Nutritional Information: Calories: 162: Fat: 9g: Carbohydrates: 20g: Protein: 2g: Sodium: 24mg: Potassium: 101mg

SPECIAL RECIPES:

BAKED FISH WITH VEGETABLES

Preparation time: 45 minutes | Serves: 4 | Cooking Time: 30 minutes

Ingredients:

- 4 (6 ounce) white fish fillets
- 1 teaspoon olive oil
- 2 teaspoons minced garlic
- 2 cups thinly sliced zucchini
- 2 cups thinly sliced yellow squash
- 1 teaspoon dried oregano
- 1 teaspoon dried thyme
- Salt and freshly ground pepper, to taste
- 1/4 cup grated Parmesan cheese

Directions:

1. Preheat the oven to 375°F.
2. Place the fish fillets in a greased baking dish.
3. In a large bowl, combine the olive oil, garlic, zucchini, yellow squash, oregano, thyme, salt, and pepper. Toss until evenly coated.
4. Spread the vegetables over the fish fillets.
5. Sprinkle the Parmesan cheese over the vegetables.
6. Bake for 30 minutes, or until the fish is cooked through and the vegetables are tender.

Nutritional Information: Calories: 186: Fat: 7g: Carbohydrates: 7g: Protein: 22g: Sodium: 128mg: Fiber: 2g

---

CONFETTI QUINOA BOWLS

Preparation Time: 20 minutes | Serves: 4 | Cooking Time: 15 minutes

Ingredients:

- 1 cup uncooked quinoa
- 2 cups vegetable broth
- 1/2 cup diced red bell pepper
- 1/2 cup diced yellow bell pepper
- 1/2 cup frozen corn
- 1/2 cup diced red onion
- 2 tablespoons olive oil
- 2 cloves garlic, minced
- Salt and pepper, to taste

Directions:

1. Bring the vegetable broth to a boil in a medium saucepan.
2. Add the quinoa and reduce the heat to low. Simmer, covered, for 15 minutes.
3. Heat the olive oil in a large skillet over medium heat.
4. Add the bell peppers, corn, onion, garlic, salt, and pepper. Cook for 5 minutes, stirring occasionally.
5. Add the cooked quinoa to the skillet and cook for an additional 5 minutes.
6. Serve warm.

Nutritional Information: Calories: 243: Fat: 8g: Carbohydrates: 36g: Protein: 6g: Sodium: 574mg: Fiber: 5g

SLOW COOKER CHICKEN AND RICE SOUP

Preparation Time: 10 minutes | Serves: 4 | Cooking Time: 6 hours

Ingredients:

- 4 cups low sodium chicken broth
- 2 cups cooked, shredded chicken
- 1 cup uncooked white rice
- 1 cup diced carrots
- 1 cup diced celery
- 1/2 cup diced onion
- 1 teaspoon minced garlic
- 2 teaspoons dried parsley
- Salt and pepper, to taste

Directions:

1. Combine all ingredients in a slow cooker.
2. Cook on low for 6 hours, stirring occasionally.
3. Serve warm.

Nutritional Information: Calories: 338: Fat: 6g: Carbohydrates: 34g: Protein: 32g: Sodium: 851mg: Fiber: 3g

---

GRILLED VEGETABLE AND BEAN SALAD

Preparation Time: 10 minutes | Serves: 4 | Cooking Time: 10 minutes

Ingredients:

- 2 cups diced zucchini
- 2 cups diced yellow squash
- 1 tablespoon olive oil
- 1/2 teaspoon dried oregano
- 1/2 teaspoon dried basil
- 1/4 teaspoon salt
- 1/4 teaspoon pepper
- 1 (15 ounce) can black beans, drained and rinsed
- 1 (15 ounce) can chickpeas, drained and rinsed
- 2 tablespoons freshly squeezed lemon juice

Directions:

1. Preheat the grill to medium high heat.
2. In a large bowl, combine the zucchini, yellow squash, olive oil, oregano, basil, salt, and pepper. Toss until evenly coated.
3. Grill the vegetables for 10 minutes, or until lightly charred.
4. In a large bowl, combine the grilled vegetables, beans, and chickpeas.
5. Drizzle with the lemon juice and toss to combine.
6. Serve warm or cold.

Nutritional Information: Calories: 233: Fat: 5g: Carbohydrates: 36g: Protein: 11g: Sodium: 336mg: Fiber: 10g

FARRO, KALE, AND MUSHROOM PILAF

Preparation Time: 20 minutes | Serves: 4 | Cooking Time: 40 minutes

Ingredients:

- 1 tablespoon olive oil
- 1/2 cup diced onion
- 1 cup uncooked farro
- 2 cups vegetable broth
- 1 cup sliced mushrooms
- 1/2 cup chopped kale
- 1 teaspoon minced garlic
- Salt and pepper, to taste

Directions:

1. Heat the olive oil in a large saucepan over medium heat.
2. Add the onion and cook for 2 minutes.
3. Add the farro and vegetable broth and bring to a boil.
4. Reduce heat to low, cover, and simmer for 30 minutes.
5. Add the mushrooms, kale, garlic, salt, and pepper. Cook for an additional 10 minutes.
6. Serve warm.

Nutritional Information: Calories: 212: Fat: 5g: Carbohydrates: 33g: Protein: 8g: Sodium: 501mg: Fiber: 5g

---

BAKED COD WITH TOMATOES AND OLIVES

Preparation Time: 10 minutes | Serves: 4 | Cooking Time: 30 minutes

Ingredients:

- 4 (6 ounce) cod fillets
- 1 tablespoon olive oil
- 1 teaspoon minced garlic
- 1 cup diced tomatoes
- 1/2 cup sliced black olives
- 1 teaspoon dried oregano
- 1 teaspoon dried thyme
- Salt and freshly ground pepper, to taste
- 2 tablespoons freshly grated Parmesan cheese

Directions:

1. Preheat the oven to 375°F.
2. Place the cod fillets in a greased baking dish.
3. In a small bowl, combine the olive oil, garlic, tomatoes, olives, oregano, thyme, salt, and pepper.
4. Spread the tomato mixture over the cod fillets.
5. Sprinkle the Parmesan cheese over the top.
6. Bake for 30 minutes, or until the cod is cooked through and the vegetables are tender.

Nutritional Information: Calories: 242: Fat: 8g: Carbohydrates: 8g: Protein: 30g: Sodium: 473mg: Fiber: 2g

ROASTED SWEET POTATO AND QUINOA BOWLS

Preparation Time: 10 minutes | Serves: 4 | Cooking Time: 30 minutes

Ingredients:

- 2 sweet potatoes, diced
- 1 tablespoon olive oil
- 1 teaspoon minced garlic
- 1 cup uncooked quinoa
- 2 cups vegetable broth
- 1/2 cup diced red bell pepper
- 1/2 cup diced yellow bell pepper
- 1/2 cup frozen corn
- 1/2 cup diced red onion
- Salt and pepper, to taste

Directions:

1. Preheat the oven to 400°F.
2. Spread the sweet potatoes in a single layer on a greased baking sheet.
3. Drizzle with the olive oil and sprinkle with the garlic, salt, and pepper.
4. Roast for 25 minutes, or until the potatoes are tender.
5. Meanwhile, bring the vegetable broth to a boil in a medium saucepan.
6. Add the quinoa and reduce the heat to low. Simmer, covered, for 15 minutes.
7. Heat the remaining olive oil in a large skillet over medium heat.
8. Add the bell peppers, corn, onion, garlic, salt, and pepper. Cook for 5 minutes, stirring occasionally.
9. Add the cooked quinoa and roasted sweet potatoes to the skillet and cook for an additional 5 minutes.
10. Serve warm.

Nutritional Information: Calories: 302: Fat: 6g: Carbohydrates: 47g: Protein: 9g: Sodium: 574mg: Fiber: 7g

---

LENTIL AND RICE STEW

Preparation Time: 10 minutes | Serves: 4 | Cooking Time: 30 minutes

Ingredients:

- 2 tablespoons olive oil
- 1/2 cup diced onion
- 1 cup uncooked white rice
- 1 cup dried lentils
- 4 cups low sodium vegetable broth
- 1 teaspoon minced garlic
- 1 teaspoon dried oregano
- 1 teaspoon dried thyme
- Salt and pepper, to taste

Directions:

1. Heat the olive oil in a large saucepan over medium heat.
2. Add the onion and cook for 3 minutes.
3. Add the rice and lentils and cook for an additional 2 minutes.
4. Add the vegetable broth, garlic, oregano, thyme, salt, and pepper.
5. Bring to a boil.
6. Reduce heat to low, cover, and simmer for 20 minutes.
7. Serve warm.

Nutritional Information: Calories: 300: Fat: 6g: Carbohydrates: 44g: Protein: 13g: Sodium: 517mg: Fiber: 8g

GRILLED EGGPLANT AND ZUCCHINI WITH FETA CHEESE

Preparation Time: 10 minutes | Serves: 4 | Cooking Time: 10 minutes

Ingredients:

- 1 large eggplant, sliced
- 1 large zucchini, sliced
- 1 tablespoon olive oil
- 1 teaspoon minced garlic
- Salt and pepper, to taste
- 1/4 cup crumbled feta cheese

Directions:

1. Preheat the grill to medium high heat.
2. In a large bowl, combine the eggplant, zucchini, olive oil, garlic, salt, and pepper. Toss until evenly coated.
3. Grill the vegetables for 10 minutes, or until lightly charred.
4. Place the grilled vegetables on a serving plate and sprinkle with the feta cheese.
5. Serve warm.

Nutritional Information: Calories: 115: Fat: 7g: Carbohydrates: 9g: Protein: 4g: Sodium: 300mg: Fiber: 4g

---

BAKED ASPARAGUS WITH PARMESAN CHEESE

Preparation Time: 10 minutes | Serves: 4 | Cooking Time: 15 minutes

Ingredients:

- 1 pound asparagus spears, trimmed
- 2 tablespoons olive oil
- 1 teaspoon minced garlic
- Salt and pepper, to taste
- 2 tablespoons freshly grated Parmesan cheese

Directions:

1. Preheat the oven to 400°F.
2. Place the asparagus in a greased baking dish.
3. Drizzle with the olive oil and sprinkle with the garlic, salt, and pepper.
4. Bake for 15 minutes, or until the asparagus is tender.
5. Sprinkle with the Parmesan cheese and serve warm.

Nutritional Information: Calories: 131: Fat: 7g: Carbohydrates: 8g: Protein: 7g: Sodium: 186mg: Fiber: 4g

ROASTED BRUSSELS SPROUTS AND SWEET POTA-TOES

Preparation Time: 10 minutes | Serves: 4 | Cooking Time: 40 minutes

Ingredients:

- 4 cups Brussels sprouts, halved
- 2 sweet potatoes, diced
- 2 tablespoons olive oil
- 1 teaspoon minced garlic
- 1 teaspoon dried oregano
- Salt and pepper, to taste

Directions:

1. Preheat the oven to 375°F.
2. Spread the Brussels sprouts and sweet potatoes in a single layer on a greased baking sheet.
3. Drizzle with the olive oil and sprinkle with the garlic, oregano, salt, and pepper.
4. Roast for 40 minutes, or until the vegetables are tender.
5. Serve warm.

Nutritional Information: Calories: 182: Fat: 7g: Carbohydrates: 26g: Protein: 5g: Sodium: 125mg: Fiber: 7g

BAKED TOFU WITH BROCCOLI AND CARROTS

Preparation Time: 10 minutes | Serves: 4 | Cooking Time: 30 minutes

Ingredients:

- 2 (14 ounce) packages extra firm tofu, cubed
- 1 tablespoon olive oil
- 1 teaspoon minced garlic
- 2 cups broccoli florets
- 2 cups shredded carrots
- 1 teaspoon dried oregano
- 1 teaspoon dried thyme
- Salt and pepper, to taste

Directions:

1. Preheat the oven to 375°F.
2. Place the tofu in a greased baking dish.
3. Drizzle with the olive oil and sprinkle with the garlic, oregano, thyme, salt, and pepper.
4. Bake for 25 minutes.
5. Add the broccoli and carrots to the baking dish and stir to combine.
6. Bake for an additional 5 minutes, or until the vegetables are tender.
7. Serve warm.

Nutritional Information: Calories: 241: Fat: 10g: Carbohydrates: 16g: Protein: 22g: Sodium: 205mg: Fiber: 5g

ROASTED CAULIFLOWER AND CHICKPEA SALAD

Preparation Time: 10 minutes | Serves: 4 | Cooking Time: 30 minutes

Ingredients:

- 1 head cauliflower, cut into florets
- 2 tablespoons olive oil
- 1 teaspoon minced garlic
- 1 (15 ounce) can chickpeas, drained and rinsed
- 1/4 cup diced red onion
- 2 tablespoons freshly squeezed lemon juice
- Salt and pepper, to taste

Directions:

1. Preheat the oven to 400°F.
2. Spread the cauliflower in a single layer on a greased baking sheet.
3. Drizzle with the olive oil and sprinkle with the garlic, salt, and pepper.
4. Roast for 25 minutes, or until the cauliflower is tender.
5. In a large bowl, combine the roasted cauliflower, chickpeas, onion, and lemon juice.
6. Toss to combine and season with salt and pepper, to taste.
7. Serve warm or cold.

Nutritional Information: Calories: 212: Fat: 6g: Carbohydrates: 30g: Protein: 10g: Sodium: 256mg: Fiber: 7g

---

BAKED SALMON WITH SPINACH AND TOMATOES

Preparation Time: 10 minutes | Serves: 4 | Cooking Time: 30 minutes

Ingredients:

- 4 (6 ounce) salmon fillets
- 1 tablespoon olive oil
- 1 teaspoon minced garlic
- 2 cups baby spinach
- 1/2 cup diced tomatoes
- 1 teaspoon dried oregano
- Salt and pepper, to taste

Directions:

1. Preheat the oven to 375°F.
2. Place the salmon fillets in a greased baking dish.
3. In a small bowl, combine the olive oil, garlic, spinach, tomatoes, oregano, salt, and pepper.
4. Spread the spinach mixture over the salmon fillets.
5. Bake for 30 minutes, or until the salmon is cooked through and the vegetables are tender.

Nutritional Information: Calories: 244: Fat: 10g: Carbohydrates: 4g: Protein: 31g: Sodium: 124mg: Fiber: 2g

FARRO AND KALE SALAD

Preparation Time: 10 minutes | Serves: 4 | Cooking Time: 25 minutes

Ingredients:

- 1 cup uncooked farro
- 2 cups vegetable broth
- 1/4 cup diced red onion
- 1/4 cup diced red bell pepper
- 1/4 cup diced yellow bell pepper
- 1/4 cup sliced black olives
- 1/4 cup crumbled feta cheese
- 2 tablespoons freshly squeezed lemon juice
- 2 tablespoons olive oil
- Salt and pepper, to taste

Directions:

1. Bring the vegetable broth to a boil in a medium saucepan.
2. Add the farro and reduce the heat to low. Simmer, covered, for 25 minutes.
3. In a large bowl, combine the cooked farro, onion, bell peppers, olives, feta cheese, lemon juice, olive oil, salt, and pepper.
4. Toss to combine.
5. Serve warm or cold.

Nutritional Information: Calories: 280: Fat: 11g: Carbohydrates: 35g: Protein: 8g: Sodium: 542mg: Fiber: 7g

---

BAKED SWEET POTATO FRIES

Preparation Time: 10 minutes | Serves: 4 | Cooking Time: 25 minutes

Ingredients:

- 4 sweet potatoes, cut into fries
- 2 tablespoons olive oil
- 1 teaspoon minced garlic
- 1 teaspoon dried oregano
- Salt and pepper, to taste

Directions:

1. Preheat the oven to 375 degrees F.
2. Line a baking sheet with parchment paper.
3. Place sweet potatoes on the baking sheet and drizzle with olive oil.
4. Sprinkle with garlic, oregano, salt and pepper.
5. Bake for 25 minutes, flipping the fries halfway through.
6. Serve hot and enjoy!

Nutritional Information: Calories: 120: Fat: 5g: Carbohydrate: 16g: Protein: 2g: Sodium: 20mg: Potassium: 320mg

SALMON SALAD

Preparation Time: 5 minutes | Serves: 4 | Cooking Time: 10 minutes

Ingredients:

- 4 (4 oz) salmon fillets
- 2 tablespoons olive oil
- 2 tablespoons lemon juice
- 2 tablespoons chopped parsley
- 1 tablespoon Dijon mustard
- Salt and pepper, to taste
- 2 cups mixed greens
- 1 cup cherry tomatoes, halved
- 1/2 cup thinly sliced red onion

Directions:

1. Heat a large skillet over medium high heat.
2. Add olive oil, then add salmon fillets.
3. Cook for about 5 minutes, flipping once.
4. Remove salmon from skillet and let cool.
5. In a small bowl, whisk together lemon juice, parsley, Dijon mustard, salt and pepper.
6. In a large bowl, combine mixed greens, tomatoes, red onion and salmon.
7. Drizzle with dressing and toss to combine.
8. Serve and enjoy!

Nutritional Information: Calories: 210: Carbohydrate: 7g: Protein: 21g: Sodium: 160mg: Potassium: 590mg

ROASTED VEGETABLE MEDLEY

Preparation Time: 10 minutes | Serves: 4 | Cooking Time: 40 minutes

Ingredients:

- 2 zucchini, chopped
- 1 red bell pepper, chopped
- 1 yellow bell pepper, chopped
- 1 onion, chopped
- 2 tablespoons olive oil
- 1 teaspoon dried oregano
- 1 teaspoon dried basil
- Salt and pepper, to taste

Directions:

1. Preheat the oven to 400 degrees F.
2. Line a baking sheet with parchment paper.
3. Place vegetables on the baking sheet and drizzle with olive oil.
4. Sprinkle with oregano, basil, salt and pepper.
5. Roast for 40 minutes, flipping once.
6. Serve and enjoy!

Nutritional Information: Calories: 110: Fat: 7g: Carbohydrate: 12g: Protein: 2g: Sodium: 20mg: Potassium: 420mg

EGGPLANT PARMESAN

Preparation Time: 10 minutes | Serves: 4 | Cooking Time: 35 minutes

Ingredients:

- 2 eggplants, sliced into 1/2 inch thick rounds
- 1/2 cup all purpose flour
- 2 eggs, lightly beaten
- 1 cup Italian style breadcrumbs
- 2 tablespoons olive oil
- 1/2 cup marinara sauce
- 1/2 cup grated Parmesan cheese

Directions:

1. Preheat the oven to 350 degrees F.
2. Line a baking sheet with parchment paper.
3. Place flour in a shallow bowl.
4. In a separate shallow bowl, combine eggs and breadcrumbs.
5. Dip eggplant slices in flour, then egg mixture, and then in breadcrumbs.
6. Place eggplant slices on the baking sheet and drizzle with olive oil.
7. Bake for 25 minutes.
8. Remove from oven and spread marinara sauce over eggplant slices.
9. Sprinkle with Parmesan cheese and bake for an additional 10 minutes.
10. Serve and enjoy!

Nutritional Information: Calories: 250: Fat: 12g: Carbohydrate: 24g: Protein: 11g: Sodium: 360mg: Potassium: 550mg

---

BAKED TILAPIA WITH BASIL PESTO

Preparation Time: 10 minutes | Serves: 4 | Cooking Time: 25 minutes

Ingredients:

- 4 (4 oz) tilapia fillets
- 2 tablespoons olive oil
- 2 tablespoons lemon juice
- 1/4 cup basil pesto
- Salt and pepper, to taste

Directions:

1. Preheat the oven to 375 degrees F.
2. Line a baking sheet with parchment paper.
3. Place tilapia fillets on the baking sheet and drizzle with olive oil and lemon juice.
4. Spread pesto over each fillet.
5. Season with salt and pepper.
6. Bake for 25 minutes, or until cooked through.
7. Serve and enjoy!

Nutritional Information: Calories: 210: Fat: 13g: Carbohydrate: 1g: Protein: 22g: Sodium: 160mg: Potassium: 450mg

QUINOA PILAF

Preparation Time: 10 minutes | Serves: 4 | Cooking Time: 25 minutes

Ingredients:

- 1 cup quinoa
- 2 cups vegetable broth
- 1 onion, diced
- 1 red bell pepper, diced
- 2 cloves garlic, minced
- 2 tablespoons olive oil
- Salt and pepper, to taste

Directions:

1. Heat a large saucepan over medium heat.
2. Add olive oil, then add onion, bell pepper and garlic.
3. Cook for about 5 minutes, stirring occasionally.
4. Add quinoa and vegetable broth and bring to a boil.
5. Reduce heat and simmer for about 20 minutes, or until quinoa is cooked through.
6. Fluff with a fork and season with salt and pepper.
7. Serve and enjoy!

Nutritional Information: Calories: 210: Fat: 8g: Carbohydrate: 24g: Protein: 6g: Sodium: 10mg: Potassium: 250mg

---

BAKED APPLES WITH CINNAMON

Preparation Time: 10 minutes | Serves: 4 | Cooking Time: 25 minutes

Ingredients:

- 4 apples, cored and sliced
- 2 tablespoons brown sugar
- 2 tablespoons butter, melted
- 1 teaspoon ground cinnamon
- 1/4 cup chopped walnuts
- 1/4 cup raisins

Directions:

1. Preheat the oven to 350 degrees F.
2. Line a baking sheet with parchment paper.
3. Place apples on the baking sheet and drizzle with melted butter.
4. Sprinkle with brown sugar, cinnamon, walnuts and raisins.
5. Bake for 25 minutes, or until apples are tender.
6. Serve and enjoy!

Nutritional Information: Calories: 160: Fat: 8g: Carbohydrate: 20g: Protein: 2g: Sodium: 10mg: Potassium: 130mg

BROCCOLI AND CAULIFLOWER CHEESE BAKE

Preparation Time: 10 minutes | Serves: 4 | Cooking Time: 25 minutes

Ingredients:

- 4 cups broccoli florets
- 4 cups cauliflower florets
- 1/4 cup butter
- 1/4 cup all purpose flour
- 2 cups milk
- 1/2 cup grated cheddar cheese
- Salt and pepper, to taste

Directions:

1. Preheat the oven to 350 degrees F.
2. Grease an 8x8 inch baking dish.
3. Place broccoli and cauliflower in the baking dish.
4. In a medium saucepan, melt butter over medium heat.
5. Whisk in flour until combined.
6. Slowly whisk in milk and cook until thickened.
7. Remove from heat and stir in cheese.
8. Pour cheese sauce over broccoli and cauliflower.
9. Bake for 25 minutes, or until vegetables are tender.
10. Serve and enjoy!

Nutritional Information: Calories: 270: Fat: 18g: Carbohydrate: 17g: Protein: 11g: Sodium: 300mg: Potassium: 500mg

---

GREEK STYLE BAKED EGGPLANT

Preparation Time: 10 minutes | Serves: 4 | Cooking Time: 30 minutes

Ingredients:

- 1 large eggplant, sliced into 1/2 inch thick rounds
- 2 tablespoons olive oil
- 1/2 cup crumbled feta cheese
- 2 tablespoons chopped fresh oregano
- 2 tablespoons chopped fresh parsley
- 2 cloves garlic, minced
- Salt and pepper, to taste

Directions:

1. Preheat the oven to 375 degrees F.
2. Line a baking sheet with parchment paper.
3. Place eggplant slices on the baking sheet and drizzle with olive oil.
4. Sprinkle with feta cheese, oregano, parsley, garlic, salt and pepper.
5. Bake for 30 minutes, flipping once.
6. Serve and enjoy!

Nutritional Information: Calories: 160: Fat: 10g: Carbohydrate: 11g: Protein: 6g: Sodium: 300mg: Potassium: 400mg

BAKED ZUCCHINI FRITTERS

Preparation Time: 10 minutes | Serves: 4 | Cooking Time: 20 minutes

Ingredients:

- 2 zucchinis, grated
- 1/4 cup all purpose flour
- 2 eggs, lightly beaten
- 1/4 cup grated Parmesan cheese
- 2 tablespoons olive oil
- Salt and pepper, to taste

Directions:

1. Preheat the oven to 375 degrees F.
2. Line a baking sheet with parchment paper.
3. Place zucchini in a large bowl and season with salt and pepper.
4. Add flour, eggs and Parmesan cheese and mix until well combined.
5. Place mixture on the baking sheet and drizzle with olive oil.
6. Bake for 20 minutes, flipping once.
7. Serve and enjoy!

Nutritional Information: Calories: 160: Fat: 9g: Carbohydrate: 9g: Protein: 8g: Sodium: 250mg: Potassium: 270mg

---

BAKED POTATO WEDGES

Preparation Time: 10 minutes | Serves: 4 | Cooking Time: 25 minutes

Ingredients:

- 4 potatoes, cut into wedges
- 2 tablespoons olive oil
- 1 teaspoon garlic powder
- 1 teaspoon onion powder
- Salt and pepper, to taste

Directions:

1. Preheat the oven to 375 degrees F.
2. Line a baking sheet with parchment paper.
3. Place potato wedges on the baking sheet and drizzle with olive oil.
4. Sprinkle with garlic powder, onion powder, salt and pepper.
5. Bake for 25 minutes, flipping once.
6. Serve and enjoy!

Nutritional Information: Calories: 130: Fat: 5g: Carbohydrate: 18g: Protein: 2g: Sodium: 10mg: Potassium: 370mg

BAKED SALMON WITH GARLIC AND HERB

Preparation Time: 10 minutes | Serves: 4 | Cooking Time: 25 minutes

Ingredients:

- 4 (4 oz) salmon fillets
- 2 tablespoons olive oil
- 1 teaspoon minced garlic
- 1 teaspoon dried thyme
- 1 teaspoon dried oregano
- Salt and pepper, to taste

Directions:

1. Preheat the oven to 375 degrees F.
2. Line a baking sheet with parchment paper.
3. Place salmon fillets on the baking sheet and drizzle with olive oil.
4. Sprinkle with garlic, thyme, oregano, salt and pepper.
5. Bake for 25 minutes, or until cooked through.
6. Serve and enjoy!

Nutritional Information: Calories: 210: Fat: 11g: Carbohydrate: 1g: Protein: 22g: Sodium: 160mg: Potassium: 450mg

---

ROASTED ASPARAGUS

Preparation Time: 10 minutes | Serves: 4 | Cooking Time: 15 minutes

Ingredients:

- 1 bunch asparagus, trimmed
- 2 tablespoons olive oil
- 1 teaspoon garlic powder
- Salt and pepper, to taste

Directions:

1. Preheat the oven to 375 degrees F.
2. Line a baking sheet with parchment paper.
3. Place asparagus on the baking sheet and drizzle with olive oil.
4. Sprinkle with garlic powder, salt and pepper.
5. Roast for 15 minutes, flipping once.
6. Serve and enjoy!

Nutritional Information: Calories: 70: Fat: 5g: Carbohydrate: 6g: Protein: 2g: Sodium: 10mg: Potassium: 260mg

BAKED SWEET POTATO CHIPS

Preparation Time: 10 minutes | Serves: 4 | Cooking Time: 25 minutes

Ingredients:

- 4 sweet potatoes, thinly sliced
- 2 tablespoons olive oil
- 1 teaspoon garlic powder
- Salt and pepper, to taste

Directions:

1. Preheat the oven to 375 degrees F.
2. Line a baking sheet with parchment paper.
3. Place sweet potato slices on the baking sheet and drizzle with olive oil.
4. Sprinkle with garlic powder, salt and pepper.
5. Bake for 25 minutes, flipping once.
6. Serve and enjoy!

Nutritional Information: Calories: 110: Fat: 5g: Carbohydrate: 16g: Protein: 2g: Sodium: 20mg: Potassium: 320mg

---

BAKED BUTTERNUT SQUASH FRIES

Preparation Time: 10 minutes | Serves: 4 | Cooking Time: 25 minutes

Ingredients:

- 4 cups cubed butternut squash
- 2 tablespoons olive oil
- 1 teaspoon dried oregano
- Salt and pepper, to taste

Directions:

1. Preheat the oven to 375 degrees F.
2. Line a baking sheet with parchment paper.
3. Place squash on the baking sheet and drizzle with olive oil.
4. Sprinkle with oregano, salt and pepper.
5. Bake for 25 minutes, flipping once.
6. Serve and enjoy!

Nutritional Information: Calories: 120: Fat: 5g: Carbohydrate: 17g: Protein: 2g: Sodium: 10mg: Potassium: 350mg

60 DAYS MEAL PLAN

DAY 1:

Breakfast: Avocado Toast with egg

Lunch: Quinoa and black bean salad

Snack: Hummus and veggie sticks

Dinner: Grilled salmon with asparagus and wild rice

Dessert: Baked apples

DAY 2:

Breakfast: Banana smoothie

Lunch: Broccoli and cheese stuffed baked potatoes

Snack: Baked sweet potato fries

Dinner: Grilled chicken and green beans

Dessert: Maple pecan oatmeal cookies

DAY 3:

Breakfast: Oatmeal with apples and walnuts

Lunch: Lentil and tomato soup

Snack: Baked zucchini fritters

Dinner: Baked salmon with roasted vegetables

Dessert: Baked peaches

DAY 4:

Breakfast: Fruit and yogurt parfait

Lunch: Baked cod with roasted vegetables

Snack: Baked kale chips

Dinner: Cheese and spinach stuffed shells

Dessert: Apple cranberry crumble

DAY 5:

Breakfast: Sweet potato hash

Lunch: Grilled vegetable and halloumi skewers

Snack: Baked eggplant fries

Dinner: Baked halibut with creamy lemon sauce

Dessert: Caramelized banana bread

DAY 6:

Breakfast: Veggie frittata

Lunch: Greek salad with chickpeas

Snack: Avocado toast

Dinner: Grilled zucchini and mushrooms

Dessert: Coconut lime custard

DAY 7:

Breakfast: Baked eggs with spinach

Lunch: Lentil and spinach salad

Snack: Baked sweet potato wedges

Dinner: Lentil and vegetable stew

Dessert: Blueberry yogurt parfait

DAY 8:

Breakfast: Breakfast burrito

Lunch: Roasted cauliflower soup

Snack: Broccoli and avocado salad

Dinner: Roasted eggplant and chickpeas

Dessert: Chocolate chip oatmeal cookies

Day 9:

Breakfast: Fruit and Yogurt Parfait

Lunch: Greek Salad with Chickpeas

Snack: Baked Sweet Potato Wedges

Dinner: Grilled Chicken and Green Beans

Dessert: Apple Cranberry Crumble

Day 10:

Breakfast: Sweet Potato Hash

Lunch: Baked Cod with Roasted Vegetables

Snack: Baked Zucchini Fritters

Dinner: Baked Tilapia with Roasted Tomatoes

Dessert: Vanilla Custard

Day 11:

Breakfast: Cottage Cheese Pancakes

Lunch: Lentil and Spinach Salad

Snack: Baked Apples

Dinner: Grilled Vegetable and Halloumi Skewers

Dessert: Banana Coconut Bread

Day 12:

Breakfast: Egg and Salsa Breakfast Wrap

Lunch: Broccoli and Cheese Stuffed Baked Potatoes

Snack: Avocado Toast

Dinner: Lentil and Vegetable Stew

Dessert: Chocolate Pudding

Day 13:

Breakfast: Veggie Frittata

Lunch: Stuffed Peppers with Lentils and Rice

Snack: Baked Tofu Fries

Dinner: Broiled Tuna Patties

Dessert: Caramelized Banana Bread

Day 14:

Breakfast: Banana Smoothie

Lunch: Roasted Cauliflower Soup

Snack: Baked Sweet Potato Fries

Dinner: Grilled Zucchini and Mushrooms

Dessert: Blueberry Yogurt Parfait

Day 15:

Breakfast: Avocado Toast with Egg

Lunch: Baked Eggplant Parmesan

Snack: Baked Kale Chips

Dinner: Baked Halibut with Creamy Lemon Sauce

Dessert: Baked Applesauce

Day 16:

Breakfast: Egg and Potato Breakfast Bowl

Lunch: Greek Salad with Chickpeas

Snack: Cucumber and Radish Salad

Dinner: Baked Tilapia with Basil Pesto

Dessert: Chocolate Peanut Butter Fudge

Day 17:

Breakfast: Baked Omelet

Lunch: Lentil and Tomato Soup

Snack: Baked Eggplant Fries

Dinner: Grilled Vegetable and Quinoa Salad

Dessert: Baked Apples with Cinnamon

Day 18:

Breakfast: Breakfast Burrito

Lunch: Baked Zucchini Fritters

Snack: Baked Falafel

Dinner: Baked Sweet Potato Fries

Dessert: Chocolate Covered Strawberries

Day 19:

Breakfast: Breakfast Tacos

Lunch: Grilled Salmon with Asparagus and Wild Rice

Snack: Broccoli and Avocado Salad

Dinner: Cheese and Spinach Stuffed Shells

Dessert: Maple Pecan Oatmeal Cookies

Day 20:

Breakfast: Breakfast Sandwich

Lunch: Quinoa and Black Bean Salad

Snack: Hummus and Veggie Sticks

Dinner: Baked Salmon with Roasted Vegetables

Dessert: Coconut Lime Custard

Day 21:

Breakfast: Oatmeal with Apples and Walnuts

Lunch: Roasted Vegetable Medley

Snack: Baked Butternut Squash

Dinner: Grilled Salmon with Asparagus and Wild Rice

Dessert: Baked Peaches

Day 22:

Breakfast: Avocado Toast with Egg

Lunch: Quinoa and Black Bean Salad

Snack: Baked Sweet Potato Fries

Dinner: Grilled Chicken and Green Beans

Dessert: Baked Apples

Day 23:

Breakfast: Egg and Salsa Breakfast Wrap

Lunch: Lentil and Tomato Soup

Snack: Baked Kale Chips

Dinner: Cheese and Spinach Stuffed Shells

Dessert: Coconut Lime Custard

Day 24:

Breakfast: Sweet Potato Hash

Lunch: Baked Cod with Roasted Vegetables

Snack: Avocado Toast

Dinner: Baked Halibut with Creamy Lemon Sauce

Dessert: Caramelized Banana Bread

Day 25:

Breakfast: Veggie Frittata

Lunch: Lentil and Spinach Salad

Snack: Hummus and Veggie Sticks

Dinner: Baked Tilapia with Roasted Tomatoes

Dessert: Apple Cranberry Crumble

Day 26:

Breakfast: Cottage Cheese Pancakes

Lunch: Greek Salad with Chickpeas

Snack: Baked Zucchini Fritters

Dinner: Roasted Vegetable Medley

Dessert: Chocolate Chip Oatmeal Cookies

Day 27:

Breakfast: Banana Smoothie

Lunch: Baked Zucchini Fritters

Snack: Baked Sweet Potato Wedges

Dinner: Roasted Eggplant and Chickpeas

Dessert: Blueberry Yogurt Parfait

Day 28:

Breakfast: Egg and Potato Breakfast Bowl

Lunch: Grilled Vegetable and Halloumi Skewers

Snack: Baked Butternut Squash

Dinner: Grilled Zucchini and Mushrooms

Dessert: Baked Peaches

Day 29:

Breakfast: Sweet Potato Hash

Lunch: Greek Salad with Chickpeas

Snack: Baked Sweet Potato Fries

Dinner: Grilled Chicken and Green Beans

Dessert: Caramelized Banana Bread

Day 30:

Breakfast: Avocado Toast with Egg

Lunch: Lentil and Spinach Salad

Snack: Baked Zucchini Fritters

Dinner: Baked Tilapia with Roasted Tomatoes

Dessert: Blueberry Yogurt Parfait

Day 31:

Breakfast: Fruit and Yogurt Parfait

Lunch: Baked Zucchini Fritters

Snack: Baked Sweet Potato Wedges

Dinner: Grilled Vegetable and Halloumi Skewers

Dessert: Baked Peaches

Day 32:

Breakfast: Cottage Cheese Pancakes

Lunch: Grilled Vegetable and Halloumi Skewers

Snack: Baked Eggplant Fries

Dinner: Roasted Vegetable Medley

Dessert: Vanilla Custard

Day 33:

Breakfast: Banana Smoothie

Lunch: Stuffed Peppers with Lentils and Rice

Snack: Baked Tofu Fries

Dinner: Grilled Zucchini and Mushrooms

Dessert: Chocolate Pudding

Day 34:

Breakfast: Egg and Potato Breakfast Bowl

Lunch: Baked Eggplant Parmesan

Snack: Avocado Toast

Dinner: Lentil and Vegetable Stew

Dessert: Banana Coconut Bread

Day 35:

Breakfast: Breakfast Burrito

Lunch: Lentil and Tomato Soup

Snack: Baked Butternut Squash

Dinner: Baked Sweet Potato Fries

Dessert: No Bake Coconut Oatmeal Bars

Day 36:

Breakfast: Breakfast Tacos

Lunch: Greek Salad with Chickpeas

Snack: Baked Falafel

Dinner: Broiled Tuna Patties

Dessert: Baked Applesauce

Day 37:

Breakfast: Breakfast Sandwich

Lunch: Lentil and Spinach Salad

Snack: Baked Falafel

Dinner: Slow Cooker Veggie Chili

Dessert: Chocolate Peanut Butter Fudge

Day 38:

Breakfast: Oatmeal with Apples and Walnuts

Lunch: Baked Cod with Roasted Vegetables

Snack: Baked Tofu Fries

Dinner: Grilled Salmon with Asparagus and Wild Rice

Dessert: Chocolate Covered Strawberries

Day 39

Breakfast: Fruit and Yogurt Parfait

Lunch: Greek Salad with Chickpeas

Snack: Baked Sweet Potato Wedges

Dinner: Baked Halibut with Creamy Lemon Sauce

Dessert: Blueberry Yogurt Parfait

Day 40

Breakfast: Cottage Cheese Pancakes

Lunch: Stuffed Peppers with Lentils and Rice

Snack: Baked Kale Chips

Dinner: Grilled Vegetable and Halloumi Skewers

Dessert: Baked Apples

Day 41

Breakfast: Egg and Salsa Breakfast Wrap

Lunch: Lentil and Spinach Salad

Snack: Hummus and Veggie Sticks

Dinner: Lentil and Vegetable Stew

Dessert: Caramelized Banana Bread

Day 42

Breakfast: Veggie Frittata

Lunch: Baked Zucchini Fritters

Snack: Baked Eggplant Fries

Dinner: Grilled Zucchini and Mushrooms

Dessert: Vanilla Custard

Day 43

Breakfast: Avocado Toast with Egg

Lunch: Grilled Salmon with Asparagus and Wild Rice

Snack: Baked Sweet Potato Fries

Dinner: Roasted Eggplant and Chickpeas

Dessert: Banana Coconut Bread

Day 44

Breakfast: Fruit and Yogurt Parfait

Lunch: Greek Salad with Chickpeas

Snack: Baked Tofu Fries

Dinner: Baked Tilapia with Roasted Tomatoes

Dessert: Chocolate Peanut Butter Fudge

Day 45

Breakfast: Cottage Cheese Pancakes

Lunch: Lentil and Tomato Soup

Snack: Broccoli and Avocado Salad

Dinner: Slow Cooker Veggie Chili

Dessert: Chocolate Covered Strawberries

Day 46

Breakfast: Egg and Broccoli Skillet

Lunch: Stuffed Peppers with Lentils and Rice

Snack: Avocado Toast

Dinner: Grilled Vegetable and Quinoa Salad

Dessert: Baked Applesauce

Day 47

Breakfast: Sweet Potato Hash

Lunch: Baked Cod with Roasted Vegetables

Snack: Baked Sweet Potato Wedges

Dinner: Broiled Tuna Patties

Dessert: Maple Pecan Oatmeal Cookies

Day 48

Breakfast: Avocado Toast with Egg

Lunch: Quinoa and Black Bean Salad

Snack: Baked Zucchini Fritters

Dinner: Grilled Chicken and Green Beans

Dessert: Apple Cranberry Crumble

Day 49

Breakfast: Fruit and Yogurt Parfait

Lunch: Greek Salad with Chickpeas

Snack: Baked Eggplant Fries

Dinner: Baked Halibut with Creamy Lemon Sauce

Dessert: Chocolate Pudding

Day 50

Breakfast: Cottage Cheese Pancakes

Lunch: Lentil and Spinach Salad

Snack: Baked Sweet Potato Fries

Dinner: Lentil and Vegetable Stew

Dessert: Caramelized Banana Bread

Day 51

Breakfast: Egg and Salsa Breakfast Wrap

Lunch: Baked Zucchini Fritters

Snack: Hummus and Veggie Sticks

Dinner: Grilled Vegetable and Halloumi Skewers

Dessert: Baked Apples

Day 52:

Breakfast: Oatmeal with Apples and Walnuts

Lunch: Grilled Salmon with Asparagus and Wild Rice

Snack: Baked Sweet Potato Fries

Dinner: Baked Salmon with Roasted Vegetables

Dessert: Caramelized Banana Bread

Day 53:

Breakfast: Baked Omelet

Lunch: Broccoli and Cheese Stuffed Baked Potatoes

Snack: Hummus and Veggie Sticks

Dinner: Grilled Chicken and Green Beans

Dessert: Baked Apples

Day 54:

Breakfast: Sweet Potato Hash

Lunch: Coconut Curry Chicken

Snack: Baked Zucchini Fritters

Dinner: Cheese and Spinach Stuffed Shells

Dessert: Coconut Lime Custard

Day 55:

Breakfast: Avocado Toast with Egg

Lunch: Spinach and Feta Frittata

Snack: Baked Sweet Potato Wedges

Dinner: Baked Halibut with Creamy Lemon Sauce

Dessert: Apple Cranberry Crumble

Day 56:

Breakfast: Fruit and Yogurt Parfait

Lunch: Quinoa and Black Bean Salad

Snack: Baked Eggplant Fries

Dinner: Baked Tilapia with Roasted Tomatoes

Dessert: Vanilla Custard

Day 57:

Breakfast: Cottage Cheese Pancakes

Lunch: Roasted Cauliflower Soup

Snack: Avocado Toast

Dinner: Roasted Vegetable Medley

Dessert: Chocolate Pudding

Day 58:

Breakfast: Banana Smoothie

Lunch: Baked Cod with Roasted Vegetables

Snack: Baked Tofu Fries

Dinner: Grilled Zucchini and Mushrooms

Dessert: Banana Coconut Bread

Day 59:

Breakfast: Egg and Potato Breakfast Bowl

Lunch: Lentil and Tomato Soup

Snack: Baked Falafel

Dinner: Lentil and Vegetable Stew

Dessert: No Bake Coconut Oatmeal Bars

Day 60:

Breakfast: Breakfast Burrito

Lunch: Baked Salmon with Mango Salsa

Snack: Baked Kale Chips

Dinner: Grilled Vegetable and Quinoa Salad

Dessert: Chocolate Peanut Butter Fudge

CONCLUSION

In conclusion, the renal diet is a critical aspect of care for individuals with kidney disease. This dietary plan can help manage the symptoms of kidney disease and slow its progression, ultimately leading to a better quality of life. The key is to focus on low sodium, low protein, and low potassium foods while also controlling portion sizes and monitoring fluid intake. The recipes outlined in this book offer a delicious and nutritious way to support the renal diet, and with 60 days of meal options, you will have plenty of variety and options to choose from. Remember to always consult with your healthcare provider to ensure that the diet is tailored to your individual needs. By incorporating the renal diet into your daily routine, you can take control of your health and live a happier and healthier life.

Made in the USA
Middletown, DE
06 October 2023

40365181R00051